WITH

Grateful Hearts

*Spiritual Reflections
for Everyday Living*

TWENTY
THIRD *23rd*
PUBLICATIONS
www.23rdpublications.com

The devotions and prayers for this book are taken from *Living Faith: Daily Catholic Devotions*, a publication of Creative Communications for the Parish, 1564 Fencorp Drive, Fenton, MO 63026.

TWENTY-THIRD PUBLICATIONS
A Division of Bayard
One Montauk Avenue, Suite 200
New London, CT 06320
(860) 437-3012 or (800) 321-0411
www.23rdpublications.com

ISBN 978-1-58595-773-6
Library of Congress Catalog Card Number: 2010921026

Cover image: ©iStockphoto.com / Martin Galabov

Printed in the U.S.A.

❧ CONTENTS ❧

EASTER

SPECIAL DAYS

ORDINARY TIME

The Right Word Just in Time

When each new issue of *Living Faith* arrived from the printer and pallet loads of copies began filling the warehouse aisles in those first years, I would scamper down to open a few bundles, inspect the cover, and flip through the pages for defects. Then I'd grab an armful of copies to hand out to colleagues.

As I stood waist-deep in *Living Faith* copies in the warehouse, it often occurred to me how presumptuous it was to have commissioned, edited, and prepared ninety-two reflections months in advance in the confident expectation that these pre-dated messages would ring true and be helpful for prayer to hundreds of thousands of readers on the very date we had assigned.

Who did we think we were, presuming to offer a few words to help a reader pray while trying to cope with a death, recovering from a serious health or other crisis, reconciling with an estranged family member, restoring (or ending) a relationship, being grateful for an unexpected blessing or any number of other urgencies?

Even more, who did we think we were to presume to offer words to help readers pray at most times when they were not faced with crises but faced with their dull and seemingly boring daily routines. My pastor once remarked that most can meet the challenges of a crisis, but many falter under the slowly grinding wheel of routine duties and chores.

This presumption behind the relevance of each dated *Living Faith* devotion was so unlike the daily newspaper journalism of my earlier career. Imagine printing daily newspapers months in advance for distribution much later on their pre-assigned dates. What would be the chances each paper would be fresh and relevant when it got to readers?

If that wasn't presumptuous enough, remember that many *Living Faith* reflections were personal sentiments about Scripture, prayer, and their Catholic faith. We could make no claims of special inspiration, theological expertise, or ecclesiastical authority (other than an imprimatur). We just did our best to share a vignette from our faith journeys clearly and concisely—in about 200 words—on every day of the year.

In the early years, I sometimes felt apologetic that *Living Faith* reflections weren't longer, more precisely focused on specific concerns at issue in the Church at the time, and more "officially" or authoritatively Catholic. Gradually it dawned on me that these reflections are helpful to so many not despite their brevity and informality but rather *because* they are brief, pointed personal sharing by ordinary Catholics about everyday difficulties and achievements in their prayer lives.

So it was always gratifying, if always a little surprising, every time we got feedback from readers thanking us for precisely the spiritual boost they needed on the very day they needed it the most. And we got that response often enough to indicate to us that many readers were finding most *Living Faith* reflections timely and relevant on most days.

Was this just-the-right-word at just-the-right-time magic? Hardly.

We were providing the prepared text, while readers, aided by the Holy Spirit, were providing the rich context of their grace-filled spiritual lives. Saint Augustine once noted that the Holy Spirit never heard a bad homily. A slight overstatement perhaps, but the basic point is sound. Inspiration is not just in the writing and the speaking of words, but in the reading and the hearing of words when read or heard.

In this sense surely it is not too presumptuous to give the Holy Spirit credit for playing a key role in the modest success of the first hundred issues of *Living Faith* during its first twenty-five years.

Thanks to the Holy Spirit and faithful readers, a good *Living Faith* reflection is both timely and timeless. This book is a collection of devotions that qualify as classic in the sense of timely when first published and timeless regardless when and how often they are read. I am as confident now that you will find this collection timely and timeless for your prayer life as I once was confident in the warehouse amid the new issues that each daily reflection would ring true and be helpful on its assigned date.

James E. Adams
Founding Editor

❧ ADVENT ❧

The Cry of the Broken-Hearted

ELIZABETH-ANNE STEWART

He has sent me to heal the broken-hearted…

Isaiah 61:1

Advent is not the season for those who are satisfied or complacent. It belongs to all who hunger for glad tidings. It holds promise for all who know themselves to be flawed. It calls us to rejoice and to hope precisely because we yearn for an alternative to life as we know it.

Advent is the season of great longing. It is the time for admitting incompleteness, inadequacy and fragmentation. It is the time for acknowledging our own woundedness and that of the world. It is never easy to confront pain. Often we feel vulnerable because praying from the center of our pain can cause emotional havoc; we can become overwhelmed by the grief which surfaces when we speak to God about our needs. It is easier to sing out in praise than to cry out for healing, but cry out we must if the God of the broken-hearted is to enter our lives.

Shelter us, Lord, in your own
wounded heart that we may find comfort.

Awake to the Marvels at Hand

FR. KENNETH E. GRABNER, CSC

> Then some of the scribes and the Pharisees said to him,
> "Teacher, we wish to see a sign from you." *Matthew 12:38*

Doesn't it seem strange that the scribes and the Pharisees asked Jesus for a sign when so many signs had already been given? Did they forget about the miraculous healing touches of Jesus that enabled the blind to see, the deaf to hear, and the lame to walk? These along with many other signs were everywhere. How did the scribes and Pharisees fail to recognize them?

God's wonders are to be found in our lives, too, and it is important that we recognize them. Can you remember experiencing unanticipated light and strength as a result of your prayer? Or feeling in a special way the enlivening presence of Jesus in the Eucharist? Can you recall the inspirations of the Holy Spirit that came to light your way when you were wandering in darkness?

We have no need of new signs to speak to us of God's power, love, and care. We need only stay awake to the marvels already given to us.

Lord, you surround me with abundant signs
of your power and care. May I be awake
to their presence in my life and thankful
for your compassionate love.

7

Don't Stifle the Joy Within You

MARY MARROCCO

...we were like men dreaming. Then our mouth was filled
with laughter, and our tongue with rejoicing.

Psalm 126:1–2

Don't be afraid to dream! Sometimes it's easier to live in a gray
world, and not let our ears hear songs and laughter. Sometimes it's a
risk to let joy, love and hope fill our hearts and color our lives. Today
God woos us, calls to the love and beauty all around and within us,
and asks us to let these take flesh.

The other day I watched two street men eating soup at a city
mission. One started to tell the other the story of Stone Soup, an
old fable. As he told it, his whole body was alive with the wonder of
the tale. As his friend listened to this child's story, his eyes began to
shine like a child's. Two dilapidated street men became radiant children, filled with wonder and awe.

Whenever we stifle or suppress the wonder and joy within us, we
hide the Kingdom. Jesus asks us instead to rejoice in the Kingdom,
rejoice in one another, and let joy fill our hearts and illuminate our
bodies. For the truth is more beautiful than our dreams, and more
joyous than the laughter of a child.

*Lord, help me become aware of the
love and beauty around me.*

Prayer for Withered Souls

ELIZABETH-ANNE STEWART

We have all withered like leaves, and our guilt carries us
away like the wind.   *Isaiah 64:5*

We have dried up, Lord. Green has turned to brown; the brilliance
of autumn reds and yellows has dulled and lost its sheen. We are
dusty and brittle, cut off from the rich sap of your presence. Wearily,
we ride upon the wind like ghosts, drifting further away from our
source with each gust. Chilled by frost and snow, cracked by blasts
of cold, we swirl in ragged abandon, caught in an endless dance of
futility. From north and south, east and west, bitterness blows, toss-
ing us from nowhere to nowhere, away from the circle of your presence whose circumference is everywhere....

O come, Lord, come! Break through the whirlwind of our despair. Silence our meaningless chattering. Save us from ourselves,
from our own worst inclinations. O come, Lord, come! Call us back
to yourself for the sake of your holy name. O come, Lord, come!
Rouse us from our apathy, from our listlessness; summon us from
the abyss. O come, Lord, come! Be our Emmanuel! Now, Lord!
Now!

Do not hide from us, O Holy One.
Do not abandon us.

9

How Suddenly Death Can Come!

MITCH FINLEY

> But God said to him, "You fool, this night your life will be demanded of you; and the things you have prepared, to whom will they belong?"
>
> *Luke 12:20*

Everyone knows of people who died suddenly, unpredictably. A father of three young children is rushed to the hospital, and three hours later he dies. A brain aneurism. Two women decide to drive to a park for a picnic. On the way, a drunk-driver's car collides with their car, and both die instantly. People get out of bed in the morning, and by the end of the day this world knows them no more. Life ended suddenly, unpredictably, in Jesus' time just as it does in our time.

Yet how much effort we put into trying to make ourselves safe and secure. Investments. Possessions. Insurance policies. Jesus knows the human heart, and he cautions us against placing too much trust in ephemeral things. Depend on one thing only, Jesus says, when push comes to shove. Depend on God alone in this world, for you are destined, sooner or later—and it could easily be "sooner"—to be with God alone, whose love for you is wider than the sky and deeper than the deepest ocean.

Loving God, help me to trust in
your love above all things.

Recovering the Stillness of Advent

ELIZABETH-ANNE STEWART

Be watchful! Be alert! You do not know when the time
will come.   *Mark 13:33*

Advent is a time for walking slowly when others are rushing, for
traveling lightly when consumers are burdened with merchandise,
for eating less when others are eating more, for focusing inward
when merrymakers drown in noisy carousing.

The season offers us the stillness that is before birth, but sad to
say, most of us cannot be still. Instead, we yield to cultural pres-
sures which urge us to begin our Christmas celebration the day
after Thanksgiving. Preoccupied with gift lists, Christmas cards and
party planning, we allow Advent, the quiet season, to become the
most frenetic time of year.

Without Advent, it is difficult to find the Christmas Christ.
When dazzled by tinsel, we cannot see the star, let alone follow it.
When speeding through the countdown before Christmas Day, we
bypass the stable. And when our ears fill with jingles about Frosty
and Rudolph, we miss the sweet strains of the angels' song...

Let your stillness blanket us, O God,
that we may be ready to celebrate
the birth of your Son.

I Need "Doses of Encouragement"

SR. JOYCE RUPP, OSM

The desert and the parched land will exult.

Isaiah 35:1

Advent Scripture passages are marvelous messengers of hope. I enjoy this liturgical season more than any other because each day I am given an opportunity to have my hope reawakened. I envision Advent as a time to let my spirit soak in the promises and pledges of Scripture. The season is an opportunity to look around and notice how God moves through my life each day as an Advocate of Hope through the positive people and situations I encounter.

During Advent I try to retune my attitudes, to see where I am stuck in life's obstacles and dissatisfactions. As I do, I uncover places in me that need a good dose of encouragement. Like a parched land exulting with new life or a deluge of rain causing a dry desert to bloom with flowers, my arid hope comes alive. I discover again that what I want to give up on actually holds the potential for future blooming and blessing.

God of hope, come to the parts
of my life that contain discontent.
Remind me that joy is not far from me.

Make Mary's Prayer Your Own

CHARLOTTE A. RANCILIO

And Mary said, "My soul proclaims the greatness of the Lord; my spirit rejoices in God my savior." *Luke 1:46–47*

Have you ever said Mary's great Magnificat as your own prayer? It is your prayer, too. You proclaim God's greatness by your very existence. You are a child of God, a friend of Jesus. God has looked upon you with great love in your weakness and, as a result, many people count you as a blessing in their lives.

God has done great things for you. Like you, Mary was no VIP in the eyes of the world; only her family and friends gave her any notice. She did ordinary, everyday things, just as you do. Yet she allowed God to dwell in her, and she began to see her life in a whole new light.

Great things happen in you, through you and to you. If you will make the first four verses of Mary's prayer your prayer, you will find that the following verses of praise will tumble from your lips and soar from your heart, just as they did from hers. God is a magnificent gift to you, and God has made you a magnificent gift to others.

Generosity Is the Heart of Faith

AMY WELBORN

> Great crowds came to him, having with them the lame,
> the blind, the deformed, the mute, and many others. They
> placed them at his feet, and he cured them. *Matthew 15:30*

I never fail to be amazed by the number of people who harbor the strong belief that this Christianity business is all about rules and restrictions. Of course, some of us who should know better probably still feel that way at times. At times.

But when we actually enter into the life of Jesus and his disciples over the centuries, what strikes us is not rules, but an overflow of lavish, extravagant love, shared with all. God's passion to reknit his broken creation is expressed in the touch of Jesus—himself the greatest gift, born in weakness, ready to embrace us if we choose.

The legends of St. Nicholas reflect this. Today we remember this kind bishop for his generosity to the poor and gift of self for the sake of his people—which, if you think about it, is a part of the story of most of the saints we honor.

In this season of gifts, I'm glad to be reminded that generosity is at the heart of faith, beginning with the gift of Jesus himself.

Preparing the Way

ELIZABETH-ANNE STEWART

Make ready the way of the Lord; clear him a straight path.

Mark 1:3

Advent is the season of the pilgrim God, the God who hungers for our love, the God who intrudes into human history by being born as one of us. We often speak of our journey toward God, but, in reality, it is God who does most of the travelling. The God who is already present in the very depths of who we are draws nearer and invites us to respond. This God insists on breaking through the wasteland into the wilderness of our hearts.

This Advent, let us make God's path smooth. Let us remove all stones and boulders, fill in potholes and treacherous pits. Let us tear down all obstacles that stand in the way, especially the overhanging branches and piles of debris from crumbling walls. And then, when this is done, let us wait, quietly and peacefully, for the One who is to come.

Remembering to "Exult in God"

SR. JOYCE RUPP, OSM

"My heart exults in the Lord."   *1 Samuel 2:1*
"My soul proclaims the greatness of the Lord."   *Luke 1:46*

Hannah and Mary begin their canticles with similar words. Each acknowledges all that the Holy One has done for her. The words of these two wonderful women seem to me the exact words I need to hear this time of year. I can get caught up in my busy world of Christmas preparations and easily miss the things for which I need to give thanks. My heart forgets to "exult in God" because I am unaware of so much that is happening. I can get caught up complaining about "how little time there is" to do all the things I want and hope to do. I become inattentive to the consistent goodness of God as revealed in people and creation around me.

So for these remaining days of Advent, I will try to awaken each morning and recommit my heart to "exulting in God" by seeing and welcoming with gratitude the numerous blessings that are mine. I will be grateful for the use of my body and mind, for the voices of those who care, for the hands and hearts that send letters of cheer and for each moment that I breathe and have life. At evening I will again "exult in God" by calling to mind the joys my day has held.

A Time to Wait

SR. RUTH MARLENE FOX, OSB

I have waited, waited for the Lord and he stooped toward
me and heard my cry. *Psalm 40:2*

So much of our life seems to be spent waiting for someone or something—waiting for Christmas, for spring, for graduation, for a sick
child to grow healthy, for a green light, for a lonely night to pass, for
the movie to begin. Some places are even set aside just for waiting—
clinic waiting rooms, train stations, checkout lines. It would be in-
teresting to calculate how much of a typical day is spent in waiting
for someone or something.

What do I do while I am waiting? Rather than pace and grow
agitated, I try to realize that this waiting time may be a gift to me, a
space in my day where I can pause and reflect on my life. Maybe it
is an opportunity for God to enter my life and remind me that I am
not in control. When I pay attention, I may hear God knocking on
my waiting time and space. My whole life is in fact a waiting time
and the world is a waiting place for God to fully enter my life.

*God, in my waiting moments this day,
may I recognize your presence.*

LENT

Looking to God for My Peace

AMY WELBORN

> Blow the trumpet Zion!
> proclaim a fast,
> call an assembly... *Joel 2:15*

To the modern eye, the ancient practice of spiritually motivated fasting seems a bit odd. How can what we do with our bodies impact our inner selves? We need look no further than the modern incarnation of fasting: The Diet. Why do we seek to lose weight, constantly and endlessly? Because of our physical health, to be sure, but for most of us, it's also about how we feel. When we're more fit, we feel more energized and better about ourselves, we say.

The fast of Lent is not about feeling better about ourselves, nor is it about losing weight. It is, however, very much about the connection between body and spirit. Self-denial teaches us that perhaps we do not need all the things we think we need. When we don't look to things to satisfy us, we are forced to look in a deeper way to God for our peace, to see that he is really all we need and to seriously evaluate how much of our material and physical satisfactions are really obstacles on our journeys to intimacy with him.

Loving God, during this lenten season,
may my physical sacrifices draw me closer to you.

A Sign That Heals and Comforts

FR. ANTHONY SCHUELLER, SSS

Make a saraph and mount it on a pole, and if anyone who
has been bitten looks at it, he will recover.   *Numbers 21:8*

When my grandmother was dying, what seemed to bring her the
most comfort was the wooden crucifix which hung in the hallway
near her bed. She would look at it for hours on end. It had been a
wedding gift many years earlier, something to help make the new
couple's house a home. My grandparents moved twice afterwards;
the crucifix always went with them and was displayed in a place
of honor. It was sign of their faith in God and a reminder of God's
closeness.

To some, the cross is a terrifying thing. For others—and I think
especially for those who suffer much or struggle with sin—it is tre-
mendously consoling. They find comfort in knowing that God's love
is so real that, in Jesus, God has embraced our human condition
and overcome evil. The crucifix, with the image of Christ lifted high
on it, spoke to my grandmother of God's closeness to her time of
need, and of victory in Jesus. I have no doubt that through it she was
healed spiritually and emotionally.

Knowing that we are not alone in our suffering and pain heals
heart and soul.

In Lent, There's No "Life as Usual"

ELIZABETH-ANNE STEWART

At once the Spirit drove him out into the desert, and he remained in the desert for forty days, tempted by Satan.

Mark 1:12–13

The impulse that led Jesus to the wilderness immediately following his baptism was powerful. The Spirit "drove him," suggesting that Jesus could not resist. After the drama of God's revelation at the river Jordan, Jesus naturally wanted solitude in which to respond to the Presence that had seized him. After all he had seen and heard, "life as usual" was an impossibility. He needed to reflect on his experience and discover where God was calling him.

Time in the desert can be terrifying. During their forty years of wandering, the Hebrew people had to encounter their "shadow side" as they struggled to move beyond infidelity and doubt. During his desert sojourn, Jesus encountered the Tempter who wanted to thwart God's work. Precisely in this wrestling with evil, we come to know God's love and mercy. This Lent, let us allow God's Spirit to blow us to those places in which we can most fully encounter ourselves; there, the work of transformation can begin.

Be with us in the desert, Lord;
save us from our fears.

Building Our Heavenly Accounts

FR. M. BASIL PENNINGTON, OCSO

Rejoice and leap for joy on that day! Behold, your reward
will be great in heaven.   *Luke 6:23*

"Woe to you, when all speak well of you." These words leave me
feeling a bit uncomfortable, for many do speak well of me. I guess
I don't appreciate enough the brethren who are quick to see my
faults and failures and limitations. Certainly, I am not at the level of
Peter and John, who were able to come forth from the Temple after
being beaten, rejoicing because they had suffered for Christ and like
Christ. But the Lord makes it easier for us lesser ones: "Rejoice and
exalt for your reward is great in heaven." There is something in it for
us. If we only have the faith to realize that everything in this world
is passing and that it is what we have in heaven that really matters,
then the slights, the hurts and insults can be seen as building up our
heavenly account and we can be happy about them.

But I would still like to grow to the stature of Peter and John, rejoicing because they were like Christ and able to suffer for him and
with him.

*Lord, increase my faith. Help me to live
in the light of eternity, to value things
in the light of heaven.*

Losing Ourselves in Service

MITCH FINLEY

For whoever wishes to save his life will lose it, but whoever loses his life for my sake will save it.   *Luke 9:24*

We spend so much time and energy trying to save our life when we
know good and well that the only way to save our life is to give it
away in service to God and neighbor. We know this—but we have
the devil's own time trying to live it. Lord, what are we to do?

At the same time, we should give ourselves credit where credit
may be due. When we give ourselves over as best we can to loving
and caring for those around us, are we not at least beginning to live
the Gospel? When we live in a family or a community that requires
us always to think of others and not just ourselves, haven't we at
least taken the first steps of "losing our life"? We work, and we pray,
and we lose sleep, and we do it for others—our family and our other
fellow pilgrims. Parents feed the hungry and clothe the naked every
day, they listen to the lonely, kiss hurts, and instruct the ignorant.
They should give themselves credit for their service to God and
neighbor. They don't think about it much, but in reflective moments
they realize that their lives are saved by the service they give.

Is Revenge Really Sweet?

FR. KENNETH E. GRABNER, CSC

I say to you, whoever is angry with his brother will be
liable to judgment. *Matthew 5:22*

A former patient of mine explained how he intended to get even
with a person who had slandered him. I pointed out that by getting
even, he would perpetuate the mutual ill will and harm himself spiritually, perhaps even physically. Why, I asked, would you put yourself in that kind of danger? He smiled and said, "Because revenge is
so sweet."

Revenge may seem to be sweet—and that is one of the reasons
why we perpetuate our enmities—but its sweetness is short-lived.
One act of revenge begets another, and the misery that ill will always
breeds only deepens.

Even more: revenge offers no lasting satisfaction because it vio-
lates who we are. God created us to live in harmony with one another because he created us in his divine image. The Father, Son, and
Holy Spirit are present to one another in a continuous outpouring
of love. When we are "in sync" with this image, we imitate God and
experience the harmony with ourselves and others that God wants
us to enjoy.

*Lord, may I be free from all ill will and so
be at peace with others and with myself.*

Is God Like an "Aching Parent"?

NANCY F. SUMMERS

> But now we must celebrate and rejoice, because your
> brother was dead and has come to life again; he was lost
> and has been found.
>
> *Luke 15:32*

The parent of a wayward child lives life in a kind of suspended animation: watching, waiting, worrying, hoping for the best, dreading the worst. Knowing that the choice to stay or return lies solely with the child is knowing powerlessness and heartbreak. Long nights are punctuated with the refrain, "Come back to me." Nothing fills the empty space in home or heart; no kind words can ease the fear that the child is dead or permanently lost.

The parent is fragmented, feeling not only the loss of the child, but surely some essential part of self as well. If the child does return, there is a relief so profound it rocks the soul. Joy is made sweeter for all the dark depths it now illuminates. One has the ability to breathe again, to envision a future again. Wholeness returns, and one celebrates.

Jesus compares God to the parent of a wayward child, and I am shocked. Such a metaphor, alternating between aching vulnerability and wild joy, is neither majestic nor dignified. Does God love us like that? I am shocked. And humbled. And grateful.

Jesus Asks Us to Drink of the Spirit

ELIZABETH-ANNE STEWART

Whoever drinks the water I shall give will never thirst.

John 4:14

We thirst for so much—not just for water but for love, for acceptance, for happiness, for self-respect, for meaning. When such thirst is left unsated, we can become depressed, embittered, angry. Just as physical thirst saps our energy, and—taken to extremes—can impair our health, so, too, spiritual thirst can be detrimental to the quality of our life. Often, we seek satisfaction in addictive behaviors, trying to numb our awareness of the thirst which grips us. And the more we seek satisfaction through inappropriate means, the more our condition deteriorates.

Jesus invites us to drink of the Spirit, the only source that will never dry up. The deeper we drink from this well, the greater our capacity to drink more. It is the fountain of life itself, water which cleanses, refreshes, renews...

Give us the water of life, Lord,
that we may never thirst again.

Following the Tug of God's Lead

JEAN ROYER

God is our refuge and our strength, an ever-present help in distress. Therefore we fear not, though the earth be shaken and mountains plunge into the depths of the sea.

Psalm 46:2–3

My little piece of "earth" has been shaken from time to time, sometimes rather severely. I have watched my "mountains" of security disappear and almost everything I found security in be swept away. The first time it happened I did not know which way to turn. Gradually, I realized that God was there, closer than my skin, and was helping me not only cope, but move ahead in a direction I had not gone before.

Since then, when life begins to change drastically, I have learned to pause in my fright, look around, look inside, and search for God's presence and loving care even in this dire circumstance. And I have never been disappointed. I may not agree with God's plan right away, and I may argue a bit, but I usually follow the lure and tug of God's lead. God always gets me where I need to be when I need to be there. Knowing I could never have found such peace on my own, I am grateful that I've followed where God led.

O Lord, help me trust even
when my earth is shaken.

Learning the Depth of God's Love

MITCH FINLEY

Can a woman forget her nursing child, or show no compassion for the child of her womb? Even these may forget, yet I will not forget you.   *Isaiah 49:15*

One of the great lessons of Lent is to grow in our awareness of the depth of God's love. When Isaiah questioned whether a woman could forget her own child, he did so because of the impossibility of the idea. For him the suggestion was preposterous. Yet we live in a different era, and recent years have seen news reports of deeply disturbed women who have not only abandoned their children but actually killed them. In one highly publicized case, a young mother put her two little sons in a car and let it roll into a lake so that her children drowned.

For Isaiah it is unthinkable that a woman would kill her own children. Yet he is willing to conceive of the notion to make a point. "Even if a mother abandons her own children," God says through Isaiah, "I will not forget you." God's love for each one of us is spectacular in its depth and lack of conditions. To grow in our appreciation of this fact is one of the great lessons of Lent.

*Loving God, help me to put
all my faith in your love.*

29

Neighbors' Weeds Are Easier to See

SR. RUTH MARLENE FOX, OSB

The Pharisees and their scribes complained to his disciples, saying, "Why do you eat and drink with tax collectors and sinners?"
Luke 5:30

No matter what Jesus said or did, it seems, the Pharisees and the scribes were always ready to find something to criticize and then pass judgment. How easy it is for them—and for us—to find faults, mistakes and bad will in others while at the same time forgetting to look in our own back yard.

A friend's four-year-old daughter was picking dandelions in front of her house and bringing them in to her parents as a bouquet. Noting that the dandelions in the yard were about ready to go to seed, her dad got the brilliant idea of offering her a penny for every dandelion she would pick. When he came home from work at the end of the day, she handed him a sack full of dandelion blossoms. But looking at his yard, he commented to her, "Why, it doesn't look like you picked any dandelions here." She replied, "I didn't. They were easier to find in our neighbor's yard."

The unwanted weeds of life are more conveniently detected in our neighbors, while our own weeds take deeper root and spread their seeds.

Jesus, help me to look for my own weeds today.

"The First Book of Revelation"

SR. JOYCE RUPP, OSM

Be holy, for I, the Lord, your God, am holy.

Leviticus 19:2

At a retreat we had a joy-filled evening of song, dance, and story-telling. The next day a participant remarked how refreshing it was to have a spiritual experience that was so much fun. She said she used to think an experience was holy only when we were thinking or speaking about God. A common misunderstanding is thinking we have to be apart from life, rather than within life, in order to be close to God. To be holy "as God is holy" is to be in union with the One who created us and loves us fully.

We have numerous opportunities to do this. Pope John Paul II commented on something similar when he visited a place of beauty in the Italian Alps. He said: "Creation is the first book of revelation." This comment reinforces the truth that the world, rather than separating us from the Holy One, can actually be a reflection of God's goodness.

Look into your life today. Where do you recognize the sacred? How is the goodness and beauty of God reflected in your own life as well as in the world around you?

"Lifting Up My Emptiness"

SR. RUTH MARLENE FOX, OSB

Standing by the cross of Jesus were his mother and his mother's sister, Mary the wife of Clopas, and Mary of Magdala.

John 19:25

Today we figuratively join Mary and the other disciples to stand by the cross with Jesus. As in other churches around the world, we will walk forward in our chapel to venerate the cross. We use a large hanging cross, so we cannot reach high enough to touch the feet of Jesus. Instead, we grasp the foot of the cross. Some touch it lightly, others clutch it for minutes as if this were their only hope.

As each one embraces the wood, I wonder what her prayer is about. Is it gratitude for Jesus' gift of himself? A request for courage to cope with cancer? A plea for healing of a family member? A cry for mercy and forgiveness? We each bring to the cross our unique and simple gift of trust and surrender. And if we feel our gift is worthless, we can take comfort from these words of the poet Jessica Powers: "If you have nothing, gather back your sigh, and with your hands held high, your heart held high, lift up your emptiness!"

Jesus, today I lift up my empty arms
to you in surrender and gratitude.

God's Rules Mean a Life Worth Living

MITCH FINLEY

> Here, then, I have today set before you life and prosperity, death and doom. If you obey the commandments of the Lord...you will live...
> *Deuteronomy 30:15–16*

Not only do we often miss the point of the individual Ten Commandments, but often we miss the point of "commandments" in general. We must admit that we don't like the idea of anyone—even God—"commanding" us to do anything. It's downright undemocratic! We should get to vote on it first!

Ah, but our Creator knows us better than we know ourselves. The point of the Ten Commandments is not to lay a bunch of arbitrary rules on us. God does not enjoy ordering us to "Jump!" because he gets a divine kick out of hearing us ask, "How high?"

Human nature is such that the Ten Commandments are standards we need to observe if we want to have a life worth living. Pure and simple. You want "life and prosperity"? Follow the Ten Commandments. You want "death and doom"? Don't follow the Ten Commandments. Simple as that.

God our loving Father, help me to live according to your way in all things.

What's the Bottom Line in My Life?

STEVE GIVENS

They exchanged their glory for the image of a grass-eating bullock. They forgot the God who had saved them, who had done great deeds in Egypt...   *Psalm 106:20–21*

Trading glory for the statue of a cow doesn't sound like a good swap, does it? How silly, we think. Who would worship a cow? Perhaps we are even ready to announce, "I'm glad I'm not like those people!"

But the real question is not "Why the cow?" but "What is my idol today?" Consider that an idol is something we give more time to than we give to God. Who among us is innocent? Where do we spend more time: at church or at work? In prayer or in front of the television? Doing good works or surfing the Internet? Helping the poor or helping ourselves to another bottle of wine?

We don't necessarily set up idols in our lives because we want to replace God. But very slowly, over the years, we do build into idols those aspects of our lives that take so much of our time and dedication. Periodically, we need to take stock and see what or who is making the rules in our lives.

Jesus, protect me from the false idols
that I create for myself.

The Promise of Rewards

SR. RUTH MARLENE FOX, OSB

...and provided you keep all his commandments, he will then raise you high in praise and renown and glory above all other nations he has made, and you will be a people sacred to the Lord, your God, as he promised.

Deuteronomy 26:18–19

We may like to think that only children are motivated by the offering of a reward, but in our daily lives as adults, we often find ourselves responding to the same system. If I please my employer, I may get a raise. If I go to visit my crabby aunt, she might remember me in her will. If I vote for this political party, they will give me a tax cut. This sounds simplistic, but surprisingly, even God uses this tactic.

We find prime examples in today's reading from Deuteronomy. If we keep God's commandments, we will be God's very own special people, a sacred people. God uses attractive motivation to help us to choose to do what is basically beneficial for our own welfare, and what will bring us happiness besides. Take time today to reflect on God's promise in this reading from Deuteronomy. See if the reward offered by God is worth the cost!

God, you claim me as your very own.
How privileged I am to belong to you.

God Wants Our Attention

FR. M. BASIL PENNINGTON, OCSO

...the house was filled with the fragrance of the oil.

John 12:3

We can almost feel a certain sympathy for poor Judas. John labels him a traitor and thief who would even rob the poor. And now he has to watch thousands of dollars worth of exquisite perfume get squandered as it pours out over the feet of Jesus and runs onto the floor. "Why this waste, this terrible waste?"

Judas is right. The perfume could have been sold for a good price. The poor could have been helped. When we sit in prayer does not the Judas, the traitor within us, cry out: "Why this waste? This time could be spent helping the poor, the needy, others."

We need to hear our Lord's defense of Mary, to know that he does indeed want us to spend time giving personal attention to him—something hard to believe, isn't it, that God could want our attention? We also need to hear John's words: The house was filled with the ointment's fragrance. When we sit in prayer the whole of the Church, the whole of the world is made more pleasing to God, is made more fragrant, a better place for us all.

Lord, give me the faith, the courage and the love
to pour myself out in prayer each day.

Guided by Mercy, Not Guilt

AMY WELBORN

Who is there like you, the God who removes guilt
and pardons sin for the remnant of his inheritance;
Who does not persist in anger forever,
but delights rather in clemency...   *Micah 7:18*

When I was five years old, I did a terrible thing. Over at a friend's house, I swiped his mother's diamond ring, right off her dresser, I believe.

The funny thing is that I remember hardly anything about the crime itself, neither the details nor, like Augustine with his pears, my motivation. What I do remember is the moment of discovery—I had worn the ring in the bathtub, it slipped off without my noticing, and my mother found it before it went on down the drain.

Yes, I remember all of that, plus the guilt I quite properly felt, and that still echoes in my consciousness decades later as I think about the act.

Sorrow for sin is, of course, a good and necessary thing, but it's a problem when guilty memories of any sin overshadows the reality of God's forgiveness. Sometimes the biggest step in faith we can make is to let that mercy, rather than our guilt, guide us.

*Lord, I'm sorry for the ways I've harmed others
and myself. Open my heart to your forgiveness.*

37

Thank God for Grace to Forgive

FR. JAMES STEPHEN BEHRENS, OCSO

...go first and be reconciled with your brother...
Matthew 5:24

Not long ago I was in a restaurant and saw a man who had once been my friend. We had enjoyed a close friendship for many years, but a painful misunderstanding kept us apart for a long time. He made the first move. He rose from the table, came over to where I was sitting and put his hand on my shoulder. With that, I rose and we hugged each other.

I told him I was sorry. He told me he was, too. And that was that. In an instant, the past was healed, and I felt so good to once again have the gift of his friendship. Forgiveness is a gift from God. I could have chosen to leave the restaurant, but I felt a hope that my friend would make the first move. Yet he really did not, for God is the Prime Mover. I thank God for inspiring my friend to come over. I thank God for letting me rise.

I know that there will be other times in my life when my stubborn nature may make me sit too long. I pray that I be open to God when those times come. He reconciles all things—with a whisper to the heart to rise and hug and begin his life in us anew.

The Shattered Dish

JAMES E. ADAMS

I am like a dish that is broken.

Psalm 31:13

This lament in Psalm 31 is surely apt for the Good Friday Passion liturgy. A more telling image of the crushed and helpless Christ facing a brutal crucifixion is hard to imagine! But this also may be a helpful lament-prayer in our less lethal personal crises.

Have you ever broken a plate from the family's only china set? If it shatters into many pieces, the sinking feeling is sharp and immediate. What was a useful and cherished part of the home becomes, in a flash, debris to be swept up. If it only breaks into two or three pieces, your grieving may be prolonged for weeks, as you toy with the misguided notion that maybe the plate can be glued together. (It can't.)

A broken dish is useless, fit only for recycling.

At times, I feel like a dish that is broken. But to make these words mine and to pray them is not to give in to despair. Rather, it's more like recognizing that something old is dead and gone, that the end of my once secure false-self is near. It is like recognizing I've hit rock-bottom, which, as the twelve-step programs teach, is when self-help and change really begin. What was once useful and cherished is now gone and needs to be recycled—and the sooner the better!

Everybody Has a Story

AMY WELBORN

...for he makes his sun rise on the bad and the good, and causes rain to fall on the just and the unjust. *Matthew 5:45*

Looking down on the earth from the window of an airplane, I am struck by the beauty and variety of the land. I'm amazed and grateful that somehow I am mysteriously (at least to me) being held aloft at such a height.

As I pass over cities and towns, I can't help but be awed and humbled by the fact that each one of the thousands of homes in my sight contains a story—or even a few—as many intricate, joyful and painful stories as there are people inside.

And God created each one of those people who are living out the stories of their lives, created them out of love. God is watching over each one, intimately involved in each life, whispering through each conscience, waiting patiently for each heart to open to his love.

I'm reminded that I'm not the center of the universe. God's love embraces all of us. And, within the limitations of my humanity, so should mine.

Lord, today I pray for those
I don't like or understand.

The High Price of Selling Out

SR. JOYCE RUPP, OSM

What are you willing to give me if I hand him over to
you? *Matthew 26:15*

When we barter away our goodness and our integrity, we pay a
price for it. Judas asked how many coins he would receive for hand-
ing Jesus over to his enemies. When we hand ourselves over to that
which is harmful for us, it depletes us of something much more
valuable than money.

I still remember in eighth grade dishonestly winning a prize
for selling magazines. No one knew I had lied except myself. In a
moment of greed and desire for recognition, I handed over what
I valued greatly: my honesty and some of my self-esteem. I lost it
by doing something that went against my better judgment. That
was a significant lesson for me in my youth. It comes back to me
when I am tempted to be less than I know I am or can be. Whether
it's speaking ill of others, exaggerating or bending the truth, being
haughty or selfish, or whatever tempts me to sell my self for something less, I remember there is a price to be paid for it.

Spirit of Love, be my guide.
Guard my integrity when
I am tempted to sell what is
precious to my soul.

Fatherly Devotion

MARK NEILSEN

> While he was still a long way off, his father caught sight of
> him and was deeply moved. *Luke 15:20*

How long had the father been waiting for his son to return? Did his eyes comb the horizon daily on the chance that the one who had left would return? What devotion kept him searching, hoping without the least sign that his child would come back? Simply as a story of the human heart, this parable is rich with suggestion and feeling.

If we understand the waiting father to be a representation of God, the story deepens. The Creator of the Universe keeping watch for one whose arrogance has led him away to squander his gifts and abuse his freedom. Even when the child is "a long way off," having as yet offered no words of repentance, God is "deeply moved."

I know I cannot understand such devotion, but I can try to believe and be glad such a God has breathed life into me, waited for me, and welcomed me back.

The Strength Faith Brings

AILEEN O'DONOGHUE

Those who are healthy do not need a physician, but the
sick do.   *Luke 5:31*

When I first went back to church after a period of atheism in my life,
I was very aware that I was doing it out of need and not any sense
of righteousness. I needed faith in a loving God to keep me from
despair. And I knew I couldn't sustain that faith without the help of
a community of believers. I need the courage and strength of faith
to face life.

Many of my friends do have the courage and strength to face life
without faith. I must admit to wondering where they get the courage. I know some of them see my practice of faith as a crutch and my
need for God as a weakness. In fact, I sometimes see it that way, too.
At those times, I can feel embarrassed just walking into church.

But I do walk in, and I stay because I know that I need to, even
when I'm not feeling either religious or sinful. It is very much like
those "regular checkups" with my physician that I know I need even
when I'm not feeling sick.

Work in Progress

MARK NEILSEN

If I do not perform my Father's works, do not believe me;
but if I perform them, even if you do not believe me, believe the works, so that you may realize [and understand]
that the Father is in me and I am in the Father.

John 10:37–38

Immediately after this confrontation with his opponents, Jesus will perform a most dramatic work: the raising of Lazarus from the dead. God seems to have accepted our need for signs and wonders, for some kind of proof and a degree of certainty. But Jesus makes clear the purpose of those works: by believing them, one might finally come around to believing in Jesus and in the Father.

Believing in a person, even a divine person, is more difficult than believing in a miracle or two. In a personal relationship, we are drawn to ever deeper trust and commitment, in good times and in bad. This is what Jesus wants of us.

But that's what we want, too, isn't it? I don't want to have to constantly prove myself by great works (as if I could!). I want friends and family to believe in me.

Most of all, I want to be sure that God loves me, regardless of my works—or the lack of them.

Turning a New Leaf

LUCIA GODWIN

Your attitude must be like that of Christ: though he was in the form of God he did not deem equality with God something to be grasped at.   *Philippians 2:5–6*

One tree in our neighborhood never seems to let go of its fall foliage. Long after the golds and reds have carpeted the lawns, this one tree holds onto its leaves tenaciously, as if to boast, "I am tree, I do not change."

It is a healthy reminder for me that change is an important part of life, and needs to be accepted. When Jesus taught, the Pharisees criticized his words because their image of God was narrow and pride-filled. They refused to change. To accept the words of Jesus would have meant letting go of their way of thinking, and no longer "grasping at" their image of God. It would have meant a change in attitude.

The curled leaves on the tree remind me to let go of my narrow views of other people, to look at them through Jesus' eyes, and to open my heart to the wind of the Spirit whose freeing touch will change my heart.

❧ EASTER ❧

Who Is Waiting for My Prayer?

SR. RUTH MARLENE FOX, OSB

> Then Peter said, "I have neither silver nor gold, but what I do have I give you: in the name of Jesus Christ the Nazorean, walk!"
>
> *Acts 3:6*

The crippled man is placed by his friends at the temple gate every day to beg for alms. Sometimes I am the person who helps another come to the temple for help; sometimes I am the helpless person who calls on others for prayer at the temple.

Recently a friend explained that she keeps a prayer album. Into this special photo album she places pictures or name tags of persons she wants to remember in prayer. Some persons might be there permanently, such as family members. Others would be there for a specific time of need. Each day at her time of prayer, she pages through the album bringing each person to her mind and into God's presence.

Someone once said that when we pray for others, we are volunteering to carry the burden or the joy of the one for whom we are praying. This is an awesome responsibility we assume when, like Peter and John, we go daily to our temple of prayer. We never know who might be at the gate waiting for our prayer.

Lord Jesus, today in my prayer I want to remember especially the following: (name them).

God Is Revealed in Everything

MARY MARROCCO

...you forgot the God who gave you birth.
Deuteronomy 32:18

Look back over the days of your life. Can you recall times, events, which led you deeper? Problems or pains you didn't understand, and perhaps still don't? Joys or sorrows, partings, meetings, unplanned by you, but woven into the fabric of your life?

Before entering the Promised Land, Moses and his people paused to recall the life they lived together. They looked back to see in their own history the ways God had been leading and teaching and loving them. They suffered very much. But in all they lived, God was intimately present. In each moment, they were learning more and more who God is. They were learning that God is present in the hearts and bodies and lives of his people. So close is the relationship between God and his beloved. In everything that happens to you, God is revealed: for God is in everything about you. Once we know this is our treasure—God's love for us—then we can leave everything else behind, joyfully and freely.

O God, let my life reveal you
in all that I am and do.

Learn to Be Untroubled of Heart

FR. JAMES MCKARNS

Do not let your hearts be troubled. You have faith in God;
have faith also in me.   *John 14:1*

Jesus may have spoken these words to people who were facing some
type of anguish or deep sorrow—perhaps a death in the family. The
message is powerful consolation to all who have a sincere trust in
the Lord's faithful love. Yet we must remember that Jesus does not
promise untroubled lives, for we will have our share of troubles that
swirl around us. But he tells us we are not to have troubled hearts.
In the center of our existence we are to remain at peace.

Picture yourself in a cozy, well-built and sealed luxury cabin high
in the mountains. It is bitter cold, and a blizzard is raging. Inside, it
is warm, quiet and peaceful, as you snuggle near the fireplace reading a book. What a difference between the inside and the outside!
The serenity inside is the way we are called to keep our hearts, Jesus
says. We are not to have troubled hearts, no matter how severe the
storms all about us. We need not have troubled hearts, if we place
our trust and hope rightly, that is, in God.

Lord, thank you for the peace
that trust in you brings.

Learning What Pleases God

SR. RUTH MARLENE FOX, OSB

Simon, son of John, do you love me?
John 21:16

Has Jesus ever asked you the question he asked Peter? If we want to be in a serious relationship with Jesus, the question will come up. Have you ever articulated your answer? Teresa of Avila said that love does not consist in pleasant and pious feelings, but rather in trying to do what pleases God.

Feelings of love come and go, like the weather. Sunny weather is wonderful, but it gives way to clouds and rain. Feelings of love can do the same, so the real test of our love for God is doing what pleases God. Then the question may come up, "How do I know what pleases God?" We can answer that with another question, "How do I know what pleases my friend, my parents, my spouse, my boss?" We learn what pleases other persons by spending time with them, by conversing with them, by reading their letters. So it is with God. We learn what pleases God by reading the Scriptures, by spending time with God each day, by reading what God's saints have written about their relationship with God.

Dear God, help me know what will be pleasing to you this very day.

A Time for "Raw and Rude Prayers"

KEVIN PERROTTA

Cast your care upon the LORD,
    and he will support you.   *Psalm 55:23*

This verse offers a comforting reassurance, but on the whole, this psalm is hardly a tranquil prayer. The psalmist "rocks with grief." He, or she, is seized with shuddering and a pounding heart because of the "clamor of the wicked," because "violence and strife" have invaded the city. It is not easy to get close to this psalmist who is so violently distraught—one minute dreaming of flying from danger like a bird, the next minute relishing the thought of watching the enemy go down "to the pit of destruction." Personally, I prefer my prayers to be more uplifting. My life has enough difficulties and frustrations, without the careening emotions of this terrified and angry psalmist.

Yet I have had my own times of rage. When my wife died. When I felt trapped in a job gone sour. I was glad then that God was willing to listen to me. He was not put off by my raw and rude prayers. He was not afraid to be close to me. If Psalm 55 is not my kind of prayer today, it is undoubtedly the prayer of many other people. I will try to pray it with them, wherever they may be.

Lord, be with those whose prayer is desperate.

Too Good to Be True?

FR. STEPHEN J. ROSSETTI

They were...incredulous for joy and were amazed...
Luke 24:41

When something really wonderful happens in our lives, we often respond with immediate incredulity: "It's too good to be true." We do not expect wonderful things for ourselves, and when they do occur, we have a difficult time accepting it.

When the risen Jesus appeared to his disciples, they were startled and afraid; they thought they were seeing a ghost. In proof that he was truly alive, Jesus let them see and touch him, and he ate a piece of fish in their midst. As they began to accept this astounding event, they were amazed and filled with joy.

One of the great obstacles to an Easter faith is our difficulty in believing that such an astounding event could happen. The risen Jesus offers us a share in his resurrected life, a life of amazement and joy. Our challenge is to believe that such a wonderful life is offered to us. For the Christian, this is not something too good to be true.

Joyful Giving

KARLA MANTERNACH

...pay your tithes in a spirit of joy.
Sirach 35:8

There was a time in my life (hard to imagine now) when I had plenty of money. Each month I would sit, pay my bills, and write checks to my parish and to whatever causes or organizations caught my interest. This was very satisfying. It made me feel rich and generous.

These days, charitable giving is more difficult. It seems like my financial obligations always outpace my resources. When money is tight, as it is for so many of us, tithing can feel more like a burden than a pleasure.

So when it is time to write those checks, I try to remember that, although I have never had all I could desire, I have always had enough—more than many others, certainly more than I have earned, probably more than I deserve. Giving is one way to show our gratitude for this. But it is also a way of imitating our God, who is total self-gift to us.

The Awesome Power of the Spirit

SR. MACRINA WIEDERKEHR, OSB

[Jesus] breathed on them and said to them, "Receive the
holy Spirit."   *John 20:22*

The doors were locked and the disciples' hearts were fearful. Fearful
hearts are locked hearts. Locked doors and locked hearts, however, were not strong enough to prevent Jesus from lovingly breaking
into their lives. Jesus breathed on his friends giving them the first
fruits of the Spirit.

Later on Pentecost Day, still lacking in power but full of hope,
these same disciples and probably others waited for the promise
to be fulfilled—the promise of receiving the fullness of the Spirit.
That they were waiting together says much about the importance
of community. With fragile hope they waited. Suddenly the joyful,
awesome sound of wind and fire arrive. Fearful hearts blossom with
courage. The barriers that came from not understanding one another burn away with the fire of the spirit.

Surely in that moment the disciples must have remembered
when Jesus came through the locked doors and breathed on them.
In the mystery of eternity, you and I were present also. Whatever
ups and downs we experience on our path of life, let us always remember the breath of the Spirit.

Darkness Defeated

ELIZABETH-ANNE STEWART

They killed him, finally, hanging him on a tree, only to have God raise him on the third day... *Acts 10:39–40*

You lived with reckless power, Lord. There was no timid tiptoeing about but bold actions done in full public view. You never stopped to think of consequences or allowed yourself to be intimidated by those conspiring against you; rather, you moved with the Spirit, proclaiming the word of life, liberating those who suffered from the grip of darkness. You were the hero, battling the monster of evil single-handedly; you were the champion of the poor, the one who spoke words of hope into aching hearts. But at the end, Lord, it seemed as though you lost. You hung on that cross like a convicted felon, bloodied and shamed...

Then, on the third day, you shattered Death and burst from the tomb; on the third day, you destroyed fear and despair. The intensity of your living not only led you to your death but also to new life. You have triumphed over all that shackles and binds, limits and constrains. Your Spirit is with us, now and always. You are Lord of the living and the dead.

Jesus Rebukes Out of Love

> Later, as the eleven were at table, he appeared to them and rebuked them for their unbelief and hardness of heart because they had not believed those who saw him after he had been raised.
>
> *Mark 16:14*

Imagine standing there right in front of Jesus, the Risen Savior, and being rebuked by him for your lack of belief and the "hardness" of your heart! Perhaps that is what purgatory is all about—looking into the face of God with no excuses, no false pretenses, no make-believe to shield you from the gaze of Love.

After all, it was love that made Jesus seek out these disciples, weak of faith and hard of heart though they were. He knew the truth about each one of them; he just wanted them to know it, too. Out of love, he rebuked them to set them free to believe in him and to proclaim the Good News of salvation to the whole world.

If your conscience sometimes rebukes you for your lack of faith and the hardness of your heart, I hope you are not discouraged. Remember the Risen Savior, the One who longs to set you free to believe and to carry the Good News to a world that is in desperate need of hope.

Learning to Trust God

SR. MARGUERITE ZRALEK, OP

Even all the hairs of your head are counted. So do not be afraid.   *Matthew 10:30–31*

I am afraid of many things. Dogs frighten me, as do heights. In spiritual matters, too, I hesitate. Although I have done some daring things in my life—pronouncing vows for instance—I always do so with apprehension. So how do I see Jesus' words, "Do not be afraid," applied to me? Given my human condition, consistent bravery seems to be impossible.

How easily I forget that Jesus' words are the ideal for which I am striving! I can improve in trust in God and in responsiveness to grace. When I look back on the past month or year, I do find some instances where I have responded to Jesus with courage. For them, I am grateful.

Matthew records that every hair of my head is counted, an image conveying how deeply God is concerned about every aspect of my well-being. Indeed, God is trustworthy—even to the point of dying for me.

Jesus, may I put my hand in your strong pierced hand
with confidence that you understand fearfulness
and still call me forward to walk with you.

The Gift of God's Presence

SR. JOYCE RUPP, OSM

Did you receive the Holy Spirit when you became
believers?
Acts 19:2

One day I walked out of the house to go to a meeting. I had my
hand on the car door, ready to open it. Suddenly a rush of peace and
well-being swept through my spirit. I immediately had this keen
awareness that someone was praying for me. I felt grateful and a bit
in awe. I knew in that moment that God was filling me with love.
This sense of an immense Power within us is one significant way in
which the Holy Spirit acts. This powerful love stirs and calls to us.
This gift of God's presence unites us and supports us. We cannot
force or control how or when this gift is given. We can only be open
and ready to receive it.

We receive the gift of the Holy Spirit when we are baptized. We
continue to receive this gracious gift each time we are open to the
goodness of God in our daily moments. It is easy to miss this graced
movement of God or to take these moments for granted. Today
might be a good day to deepen our awareness of how the Holy
Spirit guides, protects, encourages, comforts, sustains, and draws
us always toward a more whole union with our Creator.

*Holy Spirit, may I be aware of your presence and
your action in all my moments, however ordinary.*

❧ SPECIAL DAYS ❧

Mary: One of Us

January 1 • Mary, the Mother of God

SR. MELANNIE SVOBODA, SND

And Mary kept all these things, reflecting on them in her heart.

Luke 2:19

Today we celebrate not only New Year's Day, but also the Feast of Mary, the Mother of God, and the World Day of Peace.

In the chapel in our Provincial Center, we have a new life-sized statue of Mary that is unique. Mary is not standing stiffly. Rather, she is seated comfortably on a large rock. She wears no veil. Instead, her uncovered hair hangs loosely down her back. Her hands are resting on her lap; her feet are bare. Her facial expression exudes peace.

We have placed a chair in front of the statue. The chair invites people to sit down with Mary when they pray to her. When I sit in that chair to pray, something happens to me. I experience a deep sense of Mary's oneness with me, with us. I find myself saying things like, "Hi, Mary! How are you today?" And I begin effortlessly to tell her how I am.

Mary, let me never forget that you are one of us.
Please give me a reflective heart like yours!

A Biblical Model for Graceful Aging
February 2 • Presentation of the Lord

SR. MARGUERITE ZRALEK, OP

And coming forward at that very time, she gave thanks to God and spoke about the child to all who were awaiting the redemption of Jerusalem. *Luke 2:38*

By no accident did the widow Anna, eighty-four years old, happen to be in the temple to witness Simeon blessing Jesus, Mary, and Joseph. A prophetess, yes, Anna was in the right place at the right time. Now for all ages she will be known as the holy woman who thanked God for Jesus and then spread the word of his birth for the deliverance of God's people.

Widowed after only seven years of marriage—no children named in this account—Anna's life would not have been easy. And at eighty-four years, she probably found troublesome the common aches and pains of an older body. Yet she had prayed and fasted and was so attuned to God's workings that she could believe in this tiny baby. Anna could be open to the newness of God's revelation.

What an example for us as we age!

A Heart Open to God's Voice
March 19 • St. Joseph

JEAN ROYER

When Joseph awoke, he did as the angel of the Lord had commanded him and took his wife into his home.

Matthew 1:24

Joseph retired for the night having made a momentous decision—the wrong decision. He had decided on a course of action that, while humane, was not what God wanted. The angel's command—God's wish—spoke to the desire of Joseph's heart. If God wanted him to be Mary's husband, so be it. If God wanted him to raise the Son of God, so be it. Joseph would have the home and the family that God wanted him to have.

While angels may not be speaking to us in our dreams, God still speaks to our hearts in some fashion. God desires only our good, offering us deep love and care on a daily basis. God wants us to do the right thing not only because it will affect our lives, but because it will affect the lives of others as well. For our part, we need to open our hearts to God's desire for our lives.

O Lord, help me to listen well to your word spoken in my heart.

An Exemplar of Faithfulness

March 19 • St. Joseph

JEAN ROYER

The favors of the Lord I will sing forever; through all generations my mouth shall proclaim your faithfulness.

Psalm 89:2

Scripture does not record Joseph ever speaking publicly. Though his words may not have been recorded, his life "sang" eloquently of the Lord's goodness. His life sang of God's faithfulness, providence, and care for himself as well as for Mary and Jesus. So much of what Jesus learned of faithfulness must have come from what Joseph taught him.

Joseph's life speaks of God's faithfulness in keeping the covenant by sending the Messiah and by providing Joseph with all he needed to be a good foster father. As God had been faithful to him, so Joseph was faithful to God by keeping the covenant himself and by accepting all that God sent his way.

If we experience God's faithfulness as Joseph did, then we, too, will be faithful to God. Then our lives will sing of God's faithfulness, and pass that old song on to those around us and to our descendants in the faith.

Prenatal Premonition
May 31 • The Visitation of the Blessed Virgin Mary

AMY WELBORN

When Elizabeth heard Mary's greeting, the infant leaped in her womb, and Elizabeth, filled with the holy Spirit, cried out in a loud voice and said, "Most blessed are you among women, and blessed is the fruit of your womb."

Luke 1:41–42

We were all unborn children once, and in that warm darkness, we all grew, learned and, yes, listened. Any pregnant woman will tell you of the feeling she has, perhaps rooted partly in intuition and partly in hopeful, expectant imagination, that even within the womb, her child had a mind of its own. When she rests, the baby awakes and does somersaults. When heavily pregnant, she tries to move a sharp knee or elbow away from her ribs, she might just feel a push back in silent, stubborn retort.

It is the place where our lives of discernment began, where we learn for the first time, wordlessly, important truths about love, dependence, simplicity and peace. It has always intrigued and awed me that the first person to recognize Jesus as Lord was an unborn child.

Jesus, I rejoice in your presence in my life.

Loved—and Loving in Return
Sacred Heart of Jesus

SR. MARY TERESE DONZE, ASC

I kneel before the Father...that he may grant you...to know the love of Christ that surpasses knowledge.

Ephesians 3:14, 16, 19

When I was a child, a shy little boy playmate told me through my big sister, "I love you." It was as if a light turned on in my heart to learn that someone outside my family loved me. It made me feel special, and cherished for myself. It drew me beyond kinship boundaries into the wider world around me. And I loved my little friend fiercely for a whole two weeks.

That was a childish incident. But love, acknowledged and accepted, does that to us—giving a new sense of personal worth, enriching our relationships, and widening our horizons.

The love in the heart of Jesus wants to do the same for us. But there is a shyness also about Jesus' approach. He speaks to us, not directly, but through the Scriptures. He tells us of his desire for intimacy, shows himself more tender than a mother, dies to protest the genuineness of his ardor. But he waits for us to freely accept the love he offers.

What a marvel—God asking me for love! Oh, that I might accept that love, and love him fiercely in return, not for two weeks but forever.

Seeking God in My Own Heart
Immaculate Heart of Mary

MARY MARROCCO

Why were you looking for me? Did you not know that I must be in my Father's house? *Luke 2:49*

It always seemed odd to me that some of the very few recorded words of Jesus to his parents should be such sharp ones. He was only twelve. They couldn't find him and were searching for him. Why should he rebuke them? But hidden in his response is the mystery of our relationship with God. Mary and Joseph spent days seeking him. How often do we find ourselves searching for God? Sometimes he just seems absent from our lives. Other times, he seems to abandon us deliberately. We experience anxiety, anguish. Yet he lets us search, as Joseph and Mary searched. Jesus was found in the place where his Father dwells.

This is what makes the heart of Mary so clear and beautiful that we call it immaculate: she allowed God to dwell in her. She herself became God's dwelling-place, the Temple where he lives. Often when we seek God and cannot find him, it is because we are not looking in the one place where he wants us to go: inside our own heart. Let us pray for the courage to return to our own hearts and seek him there. The more he dwells in us, the more our hearts become as glorious as Mary's.

A Loving Familiarity With Jesus
July 22 • St. Mary Magdalene

SR. MELANNIE SVOBODA, SND

I have seen the Lord...

John 20:18

Called the "Apostle to the Apostles," Mary Magdalene brought the good news of Jesus' resurrection, telling the Apostles with joy and conviction, "I have seen the Lord!" Mary was witness not only to Jesus' resurrection, but also to his life, teachings, and crucifixion. Before that Easter morning, she had listened to Jesus, conversed with him, and watched helplessly as he died on the cross. This loving familiarity with Jesus enabled Mary to recognize him in the man she first mistook for the gardener.

Like Mary Magdalene, we are called to announce the good news of the gospel to others. This presupposes a loving familiarity with Jesus. It means we must listen to Jesus, converse with him, and ponder his life and teachings. It means we, like Mary Magdalene, must be able to say with joy and conviction, "I have seen the Lord!" And where do we see the Lord? We see him in the faces of our children, the hug of a friend, the smile of a stranger. We see him also in the tears of the mourner, the pleas of the homeless, the weary eyes of the refugee.

Loving Jesus, may my loving familiarity with you help me to see you in everyone I meet today.

69

The Woman of the People
August 15 • Assumption of the Blessed Virgin Mary

KEVIN PERROTTA

...a woman clothed with the sun...

Revelation 12:1

A stained-glass window in my parish church shows Mary standing on the moon, crowned with stars. To tell the truth, it is not my favorite picture of her. It makes her seem too otherworldly, too disconnected from the women around me in the pews. I prefer an icon of Mary gently cradling her Child in her arms.

While I find John's imagery strange, I do admire the way he uses it to peel back the surface of appearances. The woman who gives birth to the Messiah is, of course, both the people of Israel and the people of Christ, the Church. The long tradition that also understands the woman as Mary thus identifies Mary with the people of God. It portrays Mary as the woman of the people. The heavenly apparel reveals the woman's—the people's—heavenly dimension.

This helps me look with new eyes at the women in the pews around me. There are many "women of the people" here. In their families and jobs and wherever, they devote themselves to serving the needs of other people. John's imagery and today's feast of the women of the people enable me to detect something heavenly in their ordinariness. Already they—and us guys too—share in the life of God.

Mary Has Been Honored by God

August 22 • Queenship of the Virgin Mary

FR. M. BASIL PENNINGTON, OCSO

But many who are first will be last, and the last will be first.
Matthew 19:30

She was just a little peasant girl, they would say, nobody special in that little, lost hill town at the end of the road—there was even an adage about it: "Can anything good come out of Nazareth?" And now? She is the Queen of heaven and earth, honored from one end of the globe to the other. Indeed, venerated by the very angels of heaven and honored by God himself, who has given her a throne. "The last shall come first." How do we get to the rear of this procession? How do we become last? By giving up all that we have and all we can do and what other people think of us—all that constitutes the false self. Then God has the space to make us a somebody— "He that is mighty has done great things for me," said the humble woman from Nazareth, our glorious Queen and Mother. And then we can use the gifts God has given us to accomplish great things, knowing that all are his gift.

We honor your queenship, O holy Mother of God,
and ask your intercession that we too might show
forth the greatness of God in our lives.

The Cross: Sign of Life and Death

September 14 • The Exaltation of the Holy Cross

SR. JOYCE RUPP, OSM

He humbled himself, becoming obedient to death, even death on a cross.   *Philippians 2:8*

Death is something that most people avoid in thought and conversation. Most think it is something that happens to another person, not to themselves. Yet death is inevitable, and it is good for us to reflect upon death as part of the cycle of life. It can help us to live a much happier and whole existence by making good choices daily and by living with greater awareness and gratitude.

Jesus faced death, a most cruel death. He died as a criminal, with immense pain of body and spirit. He humbled himself, giving himself to the human process of dying that awaits us all. Death was not easy for him; his bloody sweat and anguish in the Garden of Olives tell us this. Yet in his last breath, Jesus gave a full and unconditional surrender to the One who had always been with him. His faith in the deep strength of an inner Presence helped him to give himself over to death. This same loving Presence will help us when it is our time to enter into death.

Jesus, through the power of your cross and resurrection, teach me how to live and how to die.

Our Path to Holiness
November 1 • All Saints

SR. MELANNIE SVOBODA, SND

Who may go up the mountain of the Lord?
Who can stand in his holy place?
"The clean of hand and pure of heart,
Who are not devoted to idols..."
Psalm 24:3–4

The Church sets aside the feast of All Saints to honor all those holy individuals who are not formally canonized. The responsorial psalm today gives one description of a saint: someone who is not "devoted to idols." Generally speaking, an idol is anything we worship and allow to take the place of God in our lives. Some contemporary idols might be: money, fame, power, comfort, convenience, security, pleasure, control, youthfulness.

The saints were people who worshiped God. They put their trust in neither idols nor themselves, but in God alone. Neither Superman nor Wonder Woman, the saints were ordinary individuals who became holy by staking their lives on Jesus and the Gospels. The saints show us we do not have to go far to find the path to holiness. It runs right through the circumstances of our daily lives. We find it every time we make a decision based on the teachings of Jesus.

God, help me walk the path to holiness that runs
through the circumstances of today.

Surviving Family Misunderstandings
Holy Family Sunday

MARK NEILSEN

> When his parents saw him, they were astonished, and his mother said to him, "Son, why have you done this to us? Your father and I have been looking for you with great anxiety."
>
> *Luke 2:48*

This interchange within the Holy Family is a classic of intergenerational misunderstanding. Mary focuses primarily on the distress and worry she and Joseph felt. Jesus doesn't respond to that at all, but instead rather impatiently suggests that they should have known all along where he was. That attitude, in turn, was of no help to Mary and Joseph, who "did not understand what he said to them" (verse 50).

But that's the end of it: no further recriminations were recorded, and Jesus obediently accompanied his parents back to Nazareth. Perhaps Jesus knew their concern was rooted in their love for him; perhaps he obeyed to ease their minds. For their part, Mary and Joseph carried on without fully understanding. After being initially astonished, they seem to have accepted their son for who he was becoming.

Children do astonish us, distress us, cause us anxiety. We don't always understand the things they say, but if our concern is really rooted in love, our families will grow in holiness.

❧ ORDINARY TIME ❧

Too Many Burdens

NANCY F. SUMMERS

For my yoke is easy and my burden light.

Matthew 11:30

To live the Christian life, day in and day out, often seems so hard. The struggle to be faithful, to grow in holiness, to advance in giving and forgiving, can indeed be a heavy task. The good news that Jesus' yoke is easy and his burden light appears almost absurd. We don't take our Christian vocation lightly, nor do we always find it easy!

Could it be that, in the name of faith, we have taken on yokes and burdens that were never meant for us? Do we follow a "God" who has insatiable and unrealistic standards of holiness, judges without mercy, is out of touch with human fears, limitations and needs? Are we caught up in the endless dilemma of wanting to do everything, do it right and do it all the time? Are we trying to earn salvation, just in case God's grace isn't enough? No wonder we are weary!

The Lord of Good News invites us to lay down these self-made yokes and anxiety-ridden burdens. "Come to me," he says, "and I will give you rest."

Letting Go of Our Best-Laid Plans

AMY WELBORN

The seed sown among thorns is the one who hears the word, but then worldly anxiety and the lure of riches choke the word and it bears no fruit. *Matthew 13:22*

One afternoon I looked forward to a home-cooked meal and an evening of peaceful family time. Then the fateful three o'clock hour struck. An acquaintance called and said the good stuff she was selling off before her move was going fast, and if I wanted to look, I'd better get down to her apartment. My oldest son got into the car after school and ruefully murmured, "I forgot to tell you about my basketball game tonight." Upon returning home, a cry descended from upstairs where my other son discovered his hamster had died.

Drive-through dinner, anyone? Grief counseling? A shoe box full of best-laid plans, barely used?

When we close our eyes to sleep at night, the days we reflect on are rarely the days we'd planned. This can bring us worry or even anger. At the very least, our struggle to make it through unexpected events can distract us. That needn't be the case. When we let go of our need to control and seek God in all that happens, not just in what we want to happen, we might be surprised at the fruit that grows.

A Time to Savor God's Gifts to Us

JAMES MCGINNIS

The sabbath was made for man, not man for the sabbath.
Mark 2:27

Late one summer Sunday morning, I found myself watching the birds at the various feeders in our backyard instead of turning to the chores that awaited, for we were having company that night. But it was the first time in quite a while that I had just sat and watched them. The trees that surrounded my view from the back porch swayed in the wind, their branches always reaching upward. These spires of praise were doing their prayerful thing, and I found myself praying with them. Preparation for company could come later.

It was the Sabbath, and God made the Sabbath for us—to rest and rejoice in God's creation, to savor the birds and the trees, and to savor God's presence in me and in those who would be coming to dinner later that day.

It doesn't have to be a summer morning to celebrate the Sabbath. Even in the dead of winter God has many gifts for us to savor each day. Mini-sabbatical moments each day prepare us for a weekly Sabbath to savor more fully the gifts of our lives.

We Are Each Other's Keeper

SR. MARY TERESE DONZE, ASC

Am I my brother's keeper?

Genesis 4:9

Whether we give it a thought, we are all our brother's or sister's keeper. As the poet John Donne wrote: "No man is an island." None of us can go it alone. I need you and you need me, and it is good to remember that our Father in heaven so designed it.

I sat at the breakfast table the other morning and thought of how many "brothers and sisters" of mine had made that breakfast possible. Thousands were involved in the planting, harvesting, packing, milling, selling and delivering of the grain that still had to go through hundreds of hands before it became the cereal in my bowl, the bread I ate. Thousands more had helped in the growing, picking, packing, shipping and selling of the grapefruit I enjoyed—to say nothing of the butter, coffee and milk I consumed. I marveled at the thought of the vast multitude to whom I owed that single meal. We all depend one another because, without each of us, none of us could have food, clothing, shelter.

Thank you, my brothers, my sisters.
And the most gratitude of all goes to you,
Heavenly Father, who willed that we should
thus be one another's keeper.

Learning to Lean on God

SR. JOYCE RUPP, OSM

Ask and you shall receive...

John 16:24

I am a farmer's daughter and I shall always be grateful for my childhood days on the farm. Farming holds many joys but also many sorrows. Farmers know that they cannot control the outcome of their labors. They are daily pulled into the reality of uncontrollable weather. An insect infestation, an unexpected freeze, or a drought can destroy hopes for an abundant harvest. Yet, year after year, farmers continue to plant and to trust that their work will produce something of value. Farming teaches the great need of dependence upon God. Those who work with the earth often count on the Divine Farmer to boost their spirits. Farmers know they must look to the Creator to help them accept what they cannot change and for support when they are discouraged and disappointed.

Many of you who read this will never have been on a farm, but you also have uncontrollable aspects in your life and work. You, too, have disappointing times. You, too, have to trust that if you ask you will eventually receive what you need.

All of us are dependent upon God.

The Key to the Golden Rule

JAMES E. ADAMS

> Do to others whatever you would have them do to you.
> *Matthew 7:12*

At first glance, the so-called Golden Rule of ethical behavior seems to be simple and easy. What could be simpler than knowing how you want to be treated and doing the same to others? Or avoiding doing something to others that you don't want done to you?

The trouble is, flawed as we are, we don't always want or appreciate what is best even for ourselves. We often must have the grace of God to help us recognize what we really need for our growth in the spirit rather than what we want for our convenience.

For example, if you tend to procrastinate about important decisions you need to make, you probably don't want others in your family or community to confront you about your delayed decisions. According to a simplistic reading of the Golden Rule, you would then avoid confronting others who are in a similar situation. But what is the most ethically responsible action in such a case? Likely, the truth is that the procrastinators should be confronted.

When we apply the Golden Rule, we must examine our own conscience to try to discover what God wants for us and what we really need. Then it works.

The Abuse of Religious Faith

NANCY F. SUMMERS

> Whoever comes out of the doors of my house to meet me when I return in triumph from the Ammonites shall belong to the Lord. I shall offer him up as a holocaust.
>
> *Judges 11:31*

The execution of the daughter of Jephthah is a tragedy of dramatic proportions, a sad testimony to a religion gone awry. The father commits errors that echo through the centuries as the dark underside of religion: superstition, unholy vows and violence. Through misplaced obedience to her father, the daughter even participates in her own victimhood.

The lives of these tragic figures are over, but, sadly, their era is not. At the brink of the twenty-first century, we still see religiously inspired wars and persecutions, bone-chilling fanaticism, disregard for human life in service to a "higher cause," and obedience used to manipulate and destroy.

Our first response must be to grieve, praying that we do not become immune to the horror. Then we must together find ways to stop the evil perpetrated in the name of God. Finally, each of us must face our own superstition, arrogance and victimhood. By purifying our own hearts we can help purify our world, making it less hospitable to future Jephthahs.

The Source of Our Hope

JAMES E. ADAMS

Persevere in the faith...not shifting from the hope of the gospel that you heard...   *Colossians 1:23*

In the Peace Prayer we ask to sow hope where there is despair. In some commentaries on this prayer and on helping another in despair, you see variations of this point: one can offer hope to the despairing by being with them. Our presence alone, it is suggested, is enough to turn around another's hopelessness.

We should not underestimate the good of just being with others in their despair, a spiritual work of mercy. But neither should we think that our presence alone is the source of hope. God may be using our presence to begin healing another's despair, but that is a far cry from being the source of another's hope. Unless my presence somehow points to the reality of God, then the two of us may be caught in a "blind-leading-the-blind" trap that could even deepen despair.

If healing does take place through our presence, such a situation is more likely explained by Jesus' saying that "where two or three are gathered in my name, there I am in their midst."

Lord, help me to place my hope in you alone.

Time to Grow Up

ANNE BINGHAM

The disciples approached Jesus and said, "Who is the greatest in the kingdom of heaven?"   *Matthew 18:1*

Jesus, it seems to me, was having a bit of fun when he answered the question. Like many rabbis of his time, Jesus often taught by presenting a paradox. In this case, since the disciples were acting like a bunch of kids with a serious case of sibling rivalry, I'm guessing he called over a particularly well-behaved child. The child was behaving more maturely than the supposedly adult disciples. "Shape up," Jesus was saying. "Get your priorities straight or you won't even get inside the door of the kingdom, let alone have to worry about your rank."

Remember this Gospel during difficult times. After all, even the disciples didn't "get it" all the time. When your kids are pitching a fit, it will help you avoid descending to their level and screaming back. When jockeying for position at work, this story can help you put office politics in perspective. In times of difficult parish transition, this reading can help staff and council members speak and act with compassion when there's strong reaction to painful, yet necessary, decisions.

Making Room Daily for the Spirit

FR. JAMES STEPHEN BEHRENS, OCSO

In the same way, the Spirit too comes to the aid of our weakness; for we do not know how to pray as we ought, but the Spirit itself intercedes with inexpressible groanings.

Romans 8:26

In the early morning, I walk down to a nearby lake and sit for a while. One morning recently, I thought about the day ahead and wondered how much of my formal prayer would really be prayer. Words can become routine, even those of prayer. But then I thought that perhaps the Spirit in me inspired me to go to the lake and be at peace for a while. I did pray then, asking that my words for that day be sincere, that they come from the heart and that they be all for the good. I was asking the Spirit to work in me, even though I might not be aware of it as it happens.

The life of the Spirit is a gift; I cannot control it or bargain for it. Looking out on the waters that morning, I felt some peace as I prayed to make room for the Spirit's presence that day. My life here is as good as it is God's. My words, my labors, my prayer, my groanings and my walks are his for the taking. I pray for the courage to give them to him.

*Holy Spirit, help me today and every day to
pray from the depths of my heart.*

A Tale of Divine Mercy

MARK NEILSEN

> From the roof he saw a woman bathing, who was very
> beautiful.
> *2 Samuel 11:2*

Even in an age beset by scandal, this is a story to curl your hair. At first, King David was a mere "peeping Tom," aroused by the sight of Bathsheba bathing. But then he used the considerable power of his royal office in order to have the woman brought to him for sex. Note that she was married to a soldier off fighting the king's wars. When, in the normal course of events, she became pregnant, the king, rather than accepting responsibility for what he had done, schemed to cover up the scandal. Finally, after his trickery failed, the king conspired to kill the same soldier whom he had already betrayed. Admitting the truth only after his crime was made public, David was as guilty as could be. Even his legendary penitence seems pale in comparison to what he had done.

But the wonder of this story is not about David at all; lust and cowardice and treachery are all too common in our history. The marvel is that God forgave him.

From age to age, O Lord, your mercy is without end.
Lord, may I learn to forgive as widely
and as wholeheartedly as you do.

Joy Eternal

FR. M. BASIL PENNINGTON, OCSO

...and you yourself a sword will pierce...
Luke 2:35

It is such a typically human experience. The proud young couple are filled with joy as they bring their Firstborn into the Temple. Indeed, they have a joy that none of the onlookers can even suspect, for they are bringing God's own Son into his Father's house. Their joy is compounded when a holy old man, filled with the Spirit of prophecy, comes forth to meet them and proclaims aloud their secret: God has given his People their Long-awaited.

But then comes the dire prophecy: a piercing sword for the heart of this young mother. How often in this life are not our greatest joys pierced by the realization of their transitoriness. The eternal joy that this Child came to bring us, this alone will satisfy our hearts. And it is ours only at the cost of sharing in his Cross: Take up your cross daily and follow.

Lord, we thank you for Mary our Mother and for her joy.
By the example of her sorrows may we courageously
enter into the redemption Jesus offers us.

Helping the Wayward Return

STEVE GIVENS

*...whoever brings back a sinner from the error of his way
will save his soul from death...*   *James 5:20*

How do we respond when a friend or family member falls into sin? Do we throw up our hands in exasperation and "give them enough rope to hang themselves"? Do we shrug and say, "Well, whatever turns them on"? Do we cut off our relationships with them? These all can be very human responses when we see someone we love doing things that separate them from God, the Church and us.

But we are called to higher ground than these human—and sin-filled—reactions. God wants these individuals to return home and will not rest until they return. In the words of Thérèse of Lisieux, we are the only eyes, hands, feet, mouth and heart that Christ has in this world. We are called to be shepherds for the lost sheep in our lives, watching for them, calling out to them, running after them, aching in our hearts for them and, finally, gathering them in our arms and helping them find the way back to a God who knows their failings and yet anxiously awaits their return.

*Lord, remind me that I must be Christ for all
those in my life who need most to see you.*

Praising God Is Easy to Do

MARK NEILSEN

Great is the LORD and wholly to be praised
in the city of our God.   *Psalm 48:2*

A little psalm verse like this, recited throughout the day, can transform consciousness and strengthen positive attitudes. Offering praise to God is easy: all you have to do is combine the intention to give praise with some few well-chosen words, and it begins to happen. You don't need to know how great the Lord is or how God can be wholly praised by finite creatures like us. You don't even have to know where the city of our God is: it is wherever people praise God.

Despite its simplicity, the prayer of praise, carried on at random throughout the day, has a large effect. Try it. See if your heart doesn't swell just a bit. See if gratitude doesn't come a little more easily. See if you don't discover little moments of delight that you would otherwise have overlooked.

Apparently, God enjoys our praise, stirring our hearts to experience joy and find even more reasons and opportunities to give praise.

God, thank you for the gift of praise.
Help me to nurture it in my life.

Shepherding Is Caring for Others

SR. JOYCE RUPP, OSM

I will appoint over you shepherds after my own heart,
who will shepherd you wisely...   *Jeremiah 3:15*

Who are these shepherds, described as being like God's own heart?
Shepherds are given the responsibility to care for the flock, to see
that the sheep are safe, fed, and kept from getting lost. Jesus told
his disciples that a good shepherd and the sheep always know each
other because the shepherd takes such good care of them. Ministers
of the Church are often referred to as shepherds because of their
spiritual leadership. While this is appropriate, I also think of shepherds as anyone having the privilege of caring and tending for another, whether this be spiritual or physical. Such shepherds might
be physicians with patients, parents with children, teachers with
students, counselors with clients, grandparents with grandchil-
dren, employers with employees—the list can go on and on. And
what kind of qualities are needed? The same as those in the Good
Shepherd's own heart: kindness, mercy, compassion, guidance, generosity, concern, patience, and many others.

*Shepherd of my heart, teach me how to be a
good shepherd to those whom I tend. Let my tending
be a reflection of how you care for me.*

Finding the Resources We Need

ELIZABETH-ANNE STEWART

Two hundred days' wages worth of food would not be enough for each of them to have a little [bit].   *John 6:7*

Our imaginations are too often limited by logic. As soon as a dream sparks into our consciousness, we tend to find cogent reasons for not pursuing it—not enough time, not enough money, not enough security. God presents an opportunity, and our response, more often than not, is to see insufficiency. Instead of committing ourselves to the dream, we settle for what seems more practical. The star that beckons is too far, the mountain waiting to be climbed is too high, the hungers of the world are too many.

The multiplication of the loaves and fishes demonstrates that grace is not bound by either logic or arithmetic. On perceiving a human need, Jesus does not resort to mathematical calculations to see if he can afford to feed the hungry; rather, he acts decisively, ignoring the seeming discrepancy between the number of people involved and the fragments of food available. In his presence, scarcity becomes abundance; when we turn to him in our own situations of want, we, too, will find all the resources we need to follow God's call.

Graphic Images That Shock

JAMES E. ADAMS

> So he promptly dispatched an executioner....He went off
> and beheaded him in the prison. He brought in the head
> on a platter and gave it to the girl. The girl in turn gave it
> to her mother.   *Mark 6:27–28*

Often you see warnings that this play or that display may not be
suitable for children. I've wondered if the Church should put such
a notice on this feast, which once, unashamedly, was called "The
Beheading of John." Or at least to put a caveat on the Gospel account, which tells of the part played in this sordid "adult" tale of
John's execution by Herodias' daughter, who is repeatedly referred
to as "the girl."

In recent years I've forced myself to give the shockingly vio-
lent image of a beheading free play in my imagination. What has
emerged on this feast (and others when Herod's name comes up)
are reflections about the evil of abortion, and about my own tol-
erance to focus on graphic images to remind myself that abortion
"procedures" often mean the fatal dismemberment of an individual.
If the Church has long seen fit to put such a fine point on a grue-
some beheading, I think I should acknowledge, in principle at least,
that the use of frighteningly harsh images sometimes has a valid
role to play in my personal spiritual growth.

"Under the Fig Tree"

FR. JAMES MCKARNS

Nathanael said to him, "How do you know me?" Jesus answered and said to him, "Before Philip called you, I saw you under the fig tree." *John 1:48*

Being "under the fig tree," some scholars say, means being in a state of serious thought, contemplating one's future and seeking answers to life's challenges.

It's a poetic expression.

When Jesus said he saw Nathanael under the fig tree, the meaning is that the future apostle was in prayer and thought, seeking answers for his life. Jesus connected with him, recognizing him to be a spiritual-minded seeker, intent on finding the keys to a worthwhile life. Jesus confirms that by pointing out later that there was "no guile" in Nathanael.

We, also, are to be spiritual-minded seekers of life's truths and life's holy purposes. We, too, are to spend time "under the fig tree." We do so when we participate in Mass and the sacraments, when we regularly pray, meditate, reflect on Scripture, and study the Church's teachings. When the Lord sees us "under the fig tree," he also reads our motives and invites us to share his life and love. In Jesus, Nathanael found his future; in Jesus we find ours.

The Spirit Helps Us Recognize God

AMY WELBORN

I did not know him...
John 1:31

We wander through our lives, it seems, looking for signs of God's presence. We complain that he is so difficult to find, so hard to recognize.

It might be comforting to know that we're not alone. The Scriptures are filled with stories of men and women being blind to God in their midst, looking for him in the wrong places, and being surprised by him: We need only think of Abraham's visitors and the stranger on the road to Emmaus to see that this is true.

And of John the Baptist as well, who admits to the crowd that even he, who'd been looking for and waiting didn't recognize Jesus as the Chosen One until—until what? Until the Spirit revealed him. The Spirit—not the expectations the world has taught us, nor the clues our own selfish desires would have us seek—but the Spirit of God.

Lord, open our hearts to your Spirit, so that we might recognize your presence among us.

Simeon's Prayer of Gratitude

JAMES E. ADAMS

Now, Master, you may let your servant go
   in peace, according to your word,
for my eyes have seen your salvation...   *Luke 2:29–30*

What a blessing when we all can pray Simeon's prayer of gratitude with the fervor that he prayed it! To see the Messiah, the promised One, and to recognize him confidently as our Savior and the Savior of the world—that is the goal and the crowning achievement of our Christian faith. Happy the day when we can exclaim with Simeon: "Thank you, God, I've seen it all. I've seen your incarnate Son and recognized him. I've reached the mountaintop. There's no more you need give me than this. My life is fulfilled."

No doubt, God gives some this gift in a instant. But how did Simeon come to this point? A few verses prior to his prayer, we are told that he was "righteous and devout, awaiting the consolation of Israel." Simeon had spent much of his life in longing devotion, which, we are sure, didn't earn him God's gift of faith, but surely helped prepare him to receive it when it came. So it is for most of us—we shouldn't expect Simeon's prayer to flow from our heart at the start of our journey of faith, but only after much preparation.

Thank you, God, for revealing to us your salvation.

95

Living With Death

SR. MELANNIE SVOBODA, SND

Man's days are like those of grass;
  like a flower of the field he blooms;
The wind sweeps over him and he is gone,
  and his place knows him no more.   *Psalm 103:15–16*

What is our attitude toward the sobering reality of death? Is it something we fear? Is it something we deny and avoid thinking about entirely? Or is death a reality we reflect on and pray about regularly? Do we allow the certainty of death—our own as well as that of others—to influence our decisions, determine our priorities, and color the way we relate to others? The truth is, the mystery of death can urge us to greater abandonment to God, the Giver of Life. Even our natural fear of death can lead us to greater faith in Jesus, who overcame death by rising.

As the provincial superior of a large religious community, I have seen a number of sisters die. Recently, as one of them lay dying, another sister, a good friend of hers, came into the room to pray and say her final good-bye. As she gently kissed the dying sister on the forehead, I heard her whisper, "I'll see you on the other side!"

God, Giver of Life, give me a faith-filled attitude
toward my death—and the death of others.

"A Moment of Gratitude and Humility"

MARK NEILSEN

Blessed be the name of the Lord,
    both now and forever.
From the rising to the setting of the sun
    is the name of the Lord to be praised.   *Psalm 113:2–3*

The other day as I walked out to the parking lot after work I was greeted by an immense sky filled with an unfolding sunset. Thin wisps of clouds, vapor trails from jets plus puffy clumps of cloud were all lit up in a stunning spread of color from gold to orange to pink to purple. Not being a "visual person," I have a hard time trying to describe the sight, but I suspect most of us have seen a magnificent sunrise or sunset at one time or another. Perhaps often.

I stood for a moment to take it all in, trying not to let such beauty go by without careful attention. But I quickly found I couldn't take it all in—it was just too magnificent. Even as I stood there, it gradually changed, fading here, intensifying there. This was more than I could grasp, more than I could properly appreciate. This was so clearly God's work that I could only try to soak it in before I moved on, filled, for a moment, with gratitude and humility.

Lord, may we praise your works each day.

Divine Delight

NANCY F. SUMMERS

The Lord is near to all who call upon him, to all who call upon him in truth. He fulfills the desire of those who fear him, he hears their cry and saves them.   Psalm 145:18–19

The past can haunt us: shame, regret and guilt may linger for years or even decades. We accuse ourselves in the present: "Why did I do that? How could I have been so stupid? What if I had made better choices? Wouldn't my life be wonderful if not for my past mistakes? Don't I deserve to suffer for the wrongs I have done?"

Even as we acknowledge our sins and cry out to God for relief, one last question may emerge: "How can God possibly forgive me?"

We may be tempted to think that God forgives only because it is part of God's job description! Although mercy is part of the Divine nature, we wonder if, in our case, forgiveness is dispensed only grudgingly or with many strings attached. Perhaps we need to expand or correct our understanding of who God really is. Our God forgives, not on the basis of some criteria we must satisfy, but simply and amazingly because God finds forgiving delightful. How much longer shall we deny God this joy?

Pondering God's Kindness

AMY WELBORN

O God, we ponder your kindness
within your temple.   *Psalm 48:10*

Some Sunday mornings, I seem to do everything during Mass but ponder the kindness of God, distracted continually by what I've decided are the needs of those around me. I look at my sons meaningfully, sending them telepathic threats about their posture and their participation. I soothe my daughter's hurt feelings after I whisper that no, she can't hold the baby right now, for I can see that that same baby is toddling on the edge of hysteria and will plunge right over if he's removed from my lap.

Surrounded by distractions, I can't pray. But whose fault is that? Could it be mine, since I've chosen, for that hour, to suddenly define those who are so close to the center of my life as distractions?

Perhaps I should just calm down, let my gaze rest on my own family and my parish family in gratitude, and instead of being distracted by our imperfections, choose to ponder God's kindness in placing me here.

*Lord, give me the grace to offer you
real praise for the gift of my life.*

Don't Fear, Jesus Is at the Helm

ELIZABETH-ANNE STEWART

> Meanwhile the boat, already a few miles offshore, was being tossed about by the waves, for the wind was against it. *Matthew 14:24*

If the image of Jesus walking on water reinforces our sense of his power over nature and his divinity, then the storm-tossed boat filled with terrified disciples can be said to depict our human frailty. In the early Church, in fact, this boat was regarded as a symbol of the community of the faithful: those on board are the baptized who, threatened by turbulent waters, would surely drown if Jesus were not at the helm.

The wind is often against us. Daily life presents us with personal and communal difficulties that test us at every turn. Between periods of calm, the storm hits us at full force, physically, emotionally, spiritually, financially. Whipped by wind, drenched by salt spray, we struggle to make our boat seaworthy; each loss, each challenge, brings fear, discouragement, hopelessness. Preoccupied with survival issues, we begin to lose sight of what is really important in life. Our crises, however, become God's opportunities: "Take courage, it is I; do not be afraid" (Matthew 14:27).

Climb into our boat, O Lord,
that we may be safe from all harm.

Early-Morning Brooding

FR. JAMES MCKARNS

Then he saw that they were tossed about while rowing, for the wind was against them. About the fourth watch of the night, he came toward them walking on the sea.

Mark 6:48

Jesus came to the disciples at the start of "the fourth watch," or around 3 AM. Apparently, the disciples had been struggling unsuccessfully most of the night against a stiff headwind. Jesus came to the rescue, smoothing the waves, calming their hearts and sitting down with them in the boat.

Many people seem to become unsettled during "the fourth watch," that is, very early in the morning when they can't get back to sleep, but it's just too early to get out of bed. In the darkness, problems seem to multiply and magnify. Nurses have told me that these early morning hours are often very difficult for patients in hospitals. They awaken early and begin to worry about their illnesses, families, jobs, the future.

What more apt time to invite Jesus to come to us! Even if sleep has abandoned us, Our Lord will not. Jesus will calm our fears and help us to sail peacefully into the dawn of a new day.

Lord Jesus, be with us and we will not be afraid.

"Seize the Hope Set Before Us"

ANONYMOUS

> We earnestly desire each of you to demonstrate the same
> eagerness for the fulfillment of hope...   *Hebrews 6:11*

Two decades ago, when the disease of alcoholism had me by the throat, I felt both helpless and hopeless. I was hopeless because I thought I could stop drinking on my own, but I failed again and again. The first gift that Alcoholics Anonymous gave me as I heard people tell their stories at meetings was hope. If they could get sober, so could I. Moreover, they taught me to place my hope not in myself, but in "a Power greater than ourselves" who, if sought, could and would help us.

We often mistakenly assume we need to muster up enough virtue, enough hope—or faith or love—to deserve God's help. But we don't. Instead, we need to ask God's help in everything, including that our hope may be strengthened, our hope for ourselves, for others, for this desperate world of ours. And we need to encourage one another to, in the words of AA, "seize the hope set before us" in the steadfast promises of God.

A Song of Gratitude

SR. MACRINA WIEDERKEHR, OSB

Of justice your right hand is full...
Psalm 48:11

We live in an age of turmoil; people do not feel safe. Peace, it would seem, is a beautiful word scattered through the pages of books, but where is the peace we long for? Those of us who thought we lived in peace are summoned to ask deep questions about how to bring peace to a troubled world where fear seems to be lord.

The author of Psalm 48 also lived at a time when peace was too often a stranger. This is a psalm of thanksgiving sung in the temple at a time when the people of Israel experienced a moment of joy in being delivered from their enemies. The psalmist gives praise for God's presence and support in the midst of danger.

As you pray this psalm, try to envision your own body being God's temple. Ponder God's loving kindness in the temple of your being. Sing songs of gratitude for the ways you have been rescued from dangers—both within and without.

O God, if your right hand is full of justice, then teach us to open our hands and receive from you the justice needed to create a new world. Teach us the ways of peace.

Seek Cheerfulness as a Gift of God

KEVIN PERROTTA

God loves a cheerful giver.

2 Corinthians 9:7

Well, don't we all? Who wants to have someone reluctantly agree to help and then grumble her or his way through the job? "If you can't help me without making a fuss, just forget it!" How many parents have said that to a child? It is amusing to think that God feels the same way.

Cheerful giving is mysterious to me. If helping someone is inconvenient, I almost certainly will not feel cheerful about taking the time to help. Yet it hardly seems right to beg off and say, "Sorry, can't help you. I wouldn't be cheerful, and God wouldn't be pleased." Obviously, I should help if I can—and try not to be grumpy about it. If I do help, I may be glad about it later. But I may go away feeling irritated. Helping is something I can decide to do. Feeling cheerful is not. Perhaps I should forget about it.

Yet cheerfulness cannot be dismissed as an optional extra. We are drawn to the cheerful givers and cheerful servers among us like moths to candles. We may not know where it comes from or how it works, but happiness in serving is a lovely thing, indeed, a sign of God's presence. Let us, then, seek this cheerfulness as a gift from him.

God Is Greater Than the Cosmos

AILEEN O'DONOGHUE

They seek God and wish to find him.
Wisdom 13:6

Do those seeking God in nature not find God, or is the God they find not the one they learned about in church? In packaging God for classrooms, picture books, and dashboard medallions, have we believers inadvertently made God smaller and less mysterious than the universe? I live in a particularly large universe, since my work involves studying galaxies a billion light years away. This means the light I analyze has been traveling across the emptiness of space since before life on earth evolved past algae blooms.

The God I find in this universe is much vaster and weirder than the one presented in the typical homily. I suspect that the God the homilists and the listeners know in their hearts is also vaster and weirder than words usually express. Perhaps we need to learn to speak from the depths of our hearts so seekers will see that the God we worship in church is not only larger than picture books and dashboard medallions, but larger than the universe.

Transforming Experiences

FR. JAMES KRINGS

> I have experienced much joy and encouragement from
> your love, because the hearts of the holy ones have been
> refreshed by you, brother.
>
> *Philemon 7*

My father was a veteran of World War II, and I am a cancer survivor. We both reached the same conclusion in a conversation several years ago. While we would never choose to relive our experiences, neither would we trade them away. We both believed that the transformations in each of us could not have happened any other way.

Perhaps that is why veterans in the United States gather today for parades and other events and why cancer survivors find so much encouragement, hope, and even joy from being together. Not only have we shared similar life-threatening challenges, but we are to each other what Philemon was to St. Paul: so much refreshment to our deepest hearts and selves.

Should it really take cancer or war or terrorism to have us love one another, to offer each other consolation and encouragement? Do we need to wait for something huge to befall us before we see that we are meant to be each other's refreshment through our love and compassion for one another? My father and I don't think so.

"I Forget the Largeness I'm Part of"

MARY MARROCCO

[Jesus] noticed a poor widow putting in two small coins.

Luke 21:2

Today a thunderstorm came over the lake: great chains of brilliant lightning cracking open a gray-blue horizon.

Last night, we looked up to an array of stars, untasted worlds flung across the dark sky, touching the edges of our well-trod earth.

Yesterday, I held a week-old baby, a tiny newcomer emerging out of the unknown into my arms. How small we are, and how easily we forget the largeness we are part of.

All is the Lord's, and all is contained in our God. Its unimaginable immensity is a drop of the ocean to the limitlessness that is God. Yet Jesus Christ, the One "in whom all things came to be," Lord and Master of the universe, bends low to notice two coins dropped into the collection by a most insignificant person. The greatness of his love is able to see and take in the love of a woman invisible to the world.

Lord, help me to become big enough to be
present to the little ones who need me.

Our True Riches

SR. MELANNIE SVOBODA, SND

Then [Jesus] said to the crowd, "Take care to guard against all greed, for though one may be rich, one's life does not consist of possessions."   *Luke 12:15*

When my father died, I asked for two things of his: his lunch pail and one of his plaid flannel shirts. I keep the old, metal lunch pail in a corner in my office. Every now and then I grab the handle, hold it tight for a few seconds and pray to my father. He carried that pail in his hand for decades. Now when I hold the handle, I feel I am touching my father's hand. On cool days, I wear Dad's flannel shirt around the house. I feel very close to him when I do this.

I practice these little rituals, however, not merely to feel close to my father. I do them with the hope of absorbing some of my father's spirit. Dad lived a simple life. He had few possessions. But he was rich in the things that really matter—like faith, integrity and love.

Jesus, help me to share my true
riches with others today.

Comforter

SR. JOYCE RUPP, OSM

If God is for us, who can be against us?

Romans 8:31

It took a long time for me to believe that God is for me and never against me. Not until the unexpected death of my younger brother at age twenty-three did I face the challenge of believing God is always on my side. After that death, many doubts and questions arose. How could God be for me if such intense loss came crashing into my life? If God was for my brother, why did he have to die at such an early age?

Many years later I made a thirty-day retreat in which I prayed the entire life of Jesus with his many joys and sorrows. From that experience I received the grace to see that suffering is a part of life. I came to understand and accept that God does not cause this suffering. Rather, our pain occurs because of our human condition and because life is not always fair.

God of love, when I am in the throes of life's unwanted events, comfort me and grant me the strength of a deep conviction of your abiding, caring presence.

The Majesty of the Night Stars

SR. RUTH MARLENE FOX, OSB

Yours, O Lord, are grandeur and power, majesty, splendor, and glory.

1 Chronicles 29:11

Living in a rural area offers me the privilege of viewing the majesty of the stars at night. The night sky is a display case of God's jewels. Astronomers estimate that with the naked eye a person can see about 3,000 stars, but there are 400 billion stars in the Milky Way galaxy alone. There are probably billions of galaxies! The distance and magnitude of these stars which appear in our skies call me to awesome wonder. Each night I am irresistibly drawn to my window to marvel at them. And each night I come up with only questions. What is beyond these stars? Why were they created? What is the importance of our minuscule earth in the midst of this untold splendor that God has created? What mysteries do these celestial bodies hold for us in the future?

If I cannot grasp the dimensions of nighttime space which seems to reach toward eternity, why do I even try to understand God? How incomprehensible that the stars are there and I am here! At night all I can do is gaze in awe at the sacredness of the infinite twinkling darkness, knowing that I am somehow getting a glimpse of God through my window.

God Reaches Us in Simple Ways

NANCY F. SUMMERS

> Naaman went away angry, saying, "I thought that he would surely come out and stand there to invoke the Lord his God, and would move his hand over the spot, and thus cure the leprosy."
>
> *2 Kings 5:11*

Not only did Naaman know what he wanted—cure of his leprosy—he also knew how he expected it to be done. His healing, Naaman thought, would be extraordinary and dramatic. To be told to wash seven times in the Jordan was as unspectacular as the river water itself. No spectators, no prophet, no special words and gestures. Naaman was so angry he was about to leave uncured when his servants convinced him to follow Elisha's directions.

Isn't this our story sometimes as well? When we pray, we know exactly what we want from God—healing, direction, protection, inspiration—and we want it pain-free, obvious, immediate. How little leeway we allow God! No wonder we are frequently disappointed.

God's will and purpose in our lives will be worked out for the most part in common daily circumstances, through ordinary people near at hand, in familiar signs and symbols. Part of the message of the Incarnation is that God desires to reach us through what is human, simple, and earthy.

Lord, help me see and take advantage of the simple ways by which you may be trying to heal me.

Disciples Must Not Retaliate

MARK NEILSEN

> You have heard that it was said, "An eye for an eye and a tooth for a tooth." But I say to you, offer no resistance to one who is evil.   *Matthew 5:38–39*

Why is it that most Christians don't take these words of Jesus seriously? Even many who believe in the "literal truth" of the Bible can find reason upon reason why Jesus didn't really command his followers to forsake retaliation. Why do we try to insist that Jesus either supports us or looks the other way when we attack our enemies or "get back" at those who have done us harm? His words are so clear.

I know I don't always live up to the standard Jesus sets for me in this passage and the one that follows it, requiring us to love our enemies. I doubt that I can always "turn the other cheek" or offer sincere prayer for those who are making my life miserable. And I, too, can come up with reason after reason why, this time, in this case, retaliation is called for and violence is justified.

But when I rationalize like that, I make a mistake. It is one thing to be momentarily unable to live according to God's command; it is quite another to pretend it wasn't a command at all.

Timekeeper

SR. RUTH MARLENE FOX, OSB

I tell you, brothers, the time is running out....For the world in its present form is passing away.

1 Corinthians 7:29, 31

My friend bought a new watch for herself—the old-fashioned kind with two hands, Arabic numerals and a winding stem. Each evening, she dutifully wound the watch, but noticed that the stem never grew tight as happened with her previous watches. After a year, the watch started losing time, so she returned it to the store. After inspecting it, the clerk informed her, "All it needs is a new battery."

For all those months, the wearer of the watch was convinced she was in control of the time-piece, that she kept it running with her daily ritual of winding.

In many areas of my life, I act as though I am in control of the time that is allotted to me. Even my language betrays my self-deception as I speak of "saving" time, "making" time or "wasting" time. Recognizing that I am not really in control gives me a great relief, for all the while, the unseen and unknown grace of God is directing my time from the inside.

Thank you, God, for your silent and careful creating and managing of all time.

The Gift of Contentment

JEAN ROYER

But I in justice shall behold your face; when I awake, I shall be content in your presence. *Psalm 17:15*

To be content in your presence, Lord—what a gift that is! It is what I seek. I have caught snatches of such contentment in places I least expected it and at times that seemed ill-suited for it. You have caught me unaware at times—and the delight I have felt is something I'd like to experience again and again.

To stay in this contented status constantly—wouldn't that literally be heaven! But I am mired here on earth, with all my cares and worries. Still, I need not be discouraged, because you, O Lord, are here also, closer to me than my skin, waiting for me to pay attention to your loving presence.

To have a quiet mind, eyes open to possibility, ears ready to hear your voice, I need to listen carefully for all the cues. I must be ready to change my way of expecting you, I must fit myself into the pattern of your comings and goings rather than trying to manipulate you. I must seek your presence in my life, and not be afraid to trust that you will take me where I need to be, keeping me close to you.

"Every New Ending Is a New Beginning"

TERRI MIFEK

Learn a lesson from the fig tree. When its branch becomes tender and sprouts leaves, you know that summer
is near.   *Mark 13:28*

As a resident of a northern state in the northern hemisphere, I tend
to pay close attention to the seasonal signs of change. Toward the
end of March, I begin to get a little giddy at the thought of unfro-
zen lakes, daffodils and the annual shedding of my heavy winter
jacket. Although it will be several weeks before the first buds on the
trees appear, I feel a renewed sense of hope begin to blossom in my
spirit.

As the Church Year draws to a close, we naturally think of end-
ings. The end of the world might not be uppermost in our mind, but
chances are we experienced some kind of loss this year. Perhaps a
loved one died or a dear friend moved away. Maybe we retired or
our last child moved out. Whatever we are faced with, it is important for us to not only say good-bye to what was, but to remember
that embedded in every ending is a new beginning.

*Lord, help us to recognize the signs of
hope in times of loss and emptiness.*

Opening to the Spirit

LARRY NEEB

The Spirit makes intercession for us...   *Romans 8:26*

A person who prays often opens up his vision and hope to new perspectives. For in prayer, we don't really seek to tell God what we want. He already knows that!

Rather, the purpose of prayer is to enable us to discover what we are really hoping for, what we really want. Have you ever heard of someone praying, "Lord, let Tom fall on his face this time," or "I hope Betty's reception is really a flop." Prayer is a necessary nourishment of our hope for good things.

Prayer replenishes and clarifies our lives as it helps us to believe, to seek forgiveness as well as to forgive, and to offer a blessing that comes from God at our request for others, both the lovable and the not-so-lovable.

Prayer is not a pious addition to the real world where the game is usually won by the team with the best players and not the best prayers. It is the way God uses to open the future to us, to bring about things that would otherwise not have happened. Jesus could not have gone to the cross unless he had first prayed in Gethsemane.

Lord, fill my heart with wisdom
to ask for those things I need.

A Mixed Blessing

SR. RUTH MARLENE FOX, OSB

> You will know the truth, and the truth will set you free.
>
> *John 8:32*

May God bless you with discontent at easy answers, half-truths, superficial relationships, so that you will live from deep within your heart.

May God bless you with anger at injustice, oppression, abuse and exploitation of people, so that you will work for justice, equality and peace.

May God bless you with tears to shed for those who suffer from pain, rejection, starvation and war, so that you will reach out your hand to comfort them and to change their pain to joy.

May God bless you with the foolishness to think you can make a difference in this world, so that you will do the things which others tell you cannot be done.

If you have the courage to accept these blessings, God will bless you with happiness because you will know that you have made life better for others; with inner peace because you will have worked to secure peace for others; with laughter because your heart will be light; with faithful friends because they will recognize your worth as a person.

More Good Done Than We Realize

FR. JAMES MCKARNS

But when you give alms, do not let your left hand know what your right hand is doing, so that your almsgiving may be secret. *Matthew 6:3–4*

Imagine how many good deeds are done each day that are known only to very few people.

Recently, I offered a funeral Mass for a man who was very active in our church and community. His wife later said that both she and the children were amazed how many people told of ways her husband had assisted or advised them in some way. "We knew he did a lot for others," they said, "but we probably don't know the half of it."

The daily papers and TV news reports can leave us with the feeling that people don't care for or help others as they used to, yet we need to realize that people do many good deeds for others that are unknown to the public.

Recently a spiritual author suggested that we could test our motives for doing good for others if we tell no one when we do good deeds. In that way, acts of kindness will be unselfish and spiritually motivated. They will be secrets only you and God share.

Help me, dear Lord, learn the value of doing good deeds without talking about them.

Remembering the Good in Our Life

MITCH FINLEY

The Lord then said to Abram, "I am the Lord who brought you from Ur of the Chaldeans to give you this land as a possession."

Genesis 15:7

We find it so difficult to trust in God's love for us. All we can see are the apparent darkness of the present moment. All we can see is the awful things that might happen in the future. All we can see is the grief that seems bound to overtake us given what is happening now, or what looks like will happen soon.

Abram was the same way. Even when God promised him that his dreams would come true, all Abram could see was how bleak everything looked. So God tells Abram to think back on what he has done for him already. "Look," God says, "did I not bring you from Ur of the Chaldeans 'to give you this land as a possession'? You're darn tootin' I did, so trust in me."

What worked for Abram can work for us, too. When we are anxious and afraid, we can look back on our lives at all the times our good God brought good out of what looked like an utterly bleak situation. We can recall the times that God's love has brought us through, into the light. We can do this. We can.

Loving God, help me to remember your many blessings in the past.

Awareness of Death Isn't Morbid

AMY WELBORN

Therefore, stay awake, for you know neither the day nor the hour. *Matthew 25:13*

My friend told me about her bone cancer on Halloween night. She sat on her daughter's front porch. Children's laughter drifted up and down the street in the cool darkness. "On the bone scan," she said, "my shoulder blades are black with cancer."

For days afterwards, in between my prayers, I could only wonder what it would be like—to walk through your day, knowing that an enemy was working hard within your body, and that it could win, very possibly in only a matter of months.

But, just as quickly, another thought followed. We may try to avoid it, but isn't that the way it is for all of us? Even in these days of wonder medicine, the inevitable still comes to young and old alike.

This is not to be morbid, but simply to be real—as real as the warning offered in the Gospel. We just don't know when the time will come—that moment of mystery, mixed with sadness, but ultimately filled with hope, for we trust in the Bridegroom who will come to fetch us. Are we ready?

Lord, open my heart to the meaning of my journey here on earth, and ready me for eternal life with you.

The Mysterious Seeds in Our Life

SR. RUTH MARLENE FOX, OSB

And so it happened: the earth brought forth every kind of
plant that bears seed...   *Genesis 1:11–12*

I love to hold a little seed in my hand and ponder the mystery contained in it, whether it is a dandelion seed or a carrot seed or an acorn. The blueprint for the life of the future plant is somehow mysteriously contained in the little pod resting in my hand.

There are many other mysterious seeds in our lives. One little word said to another person is the seed for the beginning or the end of a relationship. A kind deed that seems inconsequential may unfold into a whole series of meaningful events. A book casually picked up may contain the beginning of a new search for knowledge. A response to an inquiry may contain a blueprint for a new career or vocation.

Just like a carrot seed or a flower seed, each moment in our day is a seed to new experiences and new beginnings. Look carefully at all the seeds that come your way today. Ponder them, treasure them, nurture them, and wait for God's surprise when they mature.

Transformed by Love

MARK NEILSEN

> Your wife shall be like a fruitful vine
> in the recesses of your home.   *Psalm 128:3*

As the father of three wonderful children, I can be compared to many things. But one of them is not a fruitful vine. Men simply cannot bear children, no matter how much support, care and nurture they might provide. Whereas, children amazingly emerge from the very body of their mother, their father is outside the birthing process.

This marvelous situation is also a bit disconcerting: I will never have the physical intimacy of bearing a child. Instead, like all fathers, I have to decide how and to what extent I will relate to my children. And the record is mixed, both for me personally and for the race at large.

Nor is my wife entirely comfortable with the poetry of the psalms, fearing that her personhood might be reduced to her procreative function. Or to just another of her husband's possessions.

Rather than running from our human difficulties, the psalms seek to transform them by calling on the presence of God. May the parents of future generations draw strength from their unique roles as they work together to raise their children.

Index of Scripture

Index of Contributors